Multilingual Learning
stories from schools and communities in Britain

Multilingual Learning
stories from schools and communities in Britain

edited by Jean Conteh, Peter Martin
and Leena Helavaara Robertson

Trentham Books

Stoke on Trent, UK and Sterling, USA

Trentham Books Limited

Westview House	22883 Quicksilver Drive
734 London Road	Sterling
Oakhill	VA 20166-2012
Stoke on Trent	USA
Staffordshire	
England ST4 5NP	

First published 2007

British Library Cataloguing-in-Publication Data
A catalogue record for this book is available from the British Library

ISBN: 978 1 85856 398 5

Cover photograph supplied by Jean Conteh

Designed and typeset by Trentham Print Design Ltd, Chester and printed in Great Britain by Cromwell Press Ltd, Trowbridge.

Contents

The three editors have shared equally in the processes of writing the introduction and editing the contributions to this book.

Multilingual learning stories are not often told. We wish to dedicate this book to the learners, teachers and parents whose stories appear here.

Notes on contributors

Olga Barradas has a long experience as a community language teacher. Her research has focused on the academic achievement of Portuguese children. She is a visiting tutor at Goldsmiths College, University of London.

Arvind Bhatt is a research fellow at the University of East London.

Nirmala Bhojani works for Leicester City Council.

Jill Bourne is Head of the Centre for Research in Pedagogy and Curriculum and Deputy Head with responsibility for Research for the School of Education, University of Southampton.

Yangguang Chen is a visiting professor from China, currently Research Fellow in the Department of Educational Studies at Goldsmith's College, where she completed her PhD in Bilingualism in Education.

Jean Conteh is a Senior Lecturer in Primary Education at the University of Leeds. She is chair of a voluntary organisation which promotes bilingual teaching and learning in Bradford.

Angela Creese is Professor of Sociolinguistics at the University of Birmingham.

Leena Helavaara Robertson is a Principal Lecturer at Middlesex University, London. Her current research and writing focuses on multilingual early years settings and urban primary schools.

Peter Martin is Professor of Education and Linguistics at the University of East London.

Raymonde Sneddon is a teacher, teacher educator and researcher who has specialised in the language use and literacy practices of bilingual children. She is currently a visiting research fellow at the University of East London and a Trustee of the Resource Unit for Supplementary and Mother Tongue Schools.

The editors would like to acknowledge the help of Peter Conteh in organising the index.

1

Multilingual Learning Stories from Schools and Communities in Britain: issues and debates

Jean Conteh, Peter Martin and
Leena Helavaara Robertson

1. *Introduction*

This volume provides accounts of what we call 'multilingual learning stories' in schools and communities in contemporary, multilingual Britain. The detailed examples of conversations between teachers and learners bring to life children's, their parents' and their teachers' experiences of language and learning in different contexts. We provide examples from both mainstream and community settings, which illustrate the range of children's experiences as learners and show how these contribute to their identities as members of multicultural, multilingual communities. In so doing, we explore crucial issues which relate to research, policy and practice, and contribute to the debates about the meanings of multilingualism in British society.

This opening chapter has five main purposes:

- to provide a historical overview of responses in educational policy to the changing demographic profile of Britain since the Second World War. We show that, although language diversity may be recognised and celebrated in government policy, there is nevertheless a strong homogenising ideology, which creates tensions and contributes to inequality in contemporary Britain. These tensions are clearly revealed in the specific stories told in the following chapters.

■ to show some of the ways in which different communities have responded to these policies in order to overcome the inequalities underpinning them. Each chapter illustrates the ways in which a particular community has actively engaged with the inequalities, constructing specific teaching and learning spaces that fit their own individual circumstances.

■ to suggest theoretical frameworks which help to explain the multilingual stories the book tells. It is important to understand the finegrained detail of the conversations which make up the stories as well as the wider historical, political and social contexts in which they are situated. It also illustrates research methodologies which will enable us to reveal and understand multilingual learning stories as yet untold.

■ to raise a key issue in the changing field of understanding learning in contemporary multilingual Britain – that of terminology. We recognise the powerful ideological messages embedded in particular terms used to describe different learning contexts and the actors within them and hope to contribute to the ongoing discussions in this area.

■ to provide brief overviews of each chapter.

1.1 *The historical context*

It is not possible in a short introductory chapter to provide a full account of all the policies enacted over the past fifty years or so which relate to the rapidly changing demography of Britain. Table One (page 21) provides a chronological list of those which map responses to language diversity and the development of community schooling. In this section, we discuss them thematically to draw out the somewhat contradictory responses to multilingualism in schools and the development of the curriculum in Britain.

1.2 *Responses to multilingualism*

The report *English for Immigrants* (DES, 1963) was possibly the first to recognise that the growing numbers of arrivals from South Asia, the Caribbean and other former British colonies had implications for language and education. It was grounded in a policy of assimilation. 'Immigrant' pupils – as they were known – were to be withdrawn from mainstream classes for separate English lessons until they could operate in the new language at a satisfactory level. This was soon followed in 1966 by the Local Government Act, Section 11, which stipulated that schools with large proportions of immigrant children were to be offered extra financial support. Teachers engaging in what was called 'language support' work became known as 'Section 11 teachers'. For more than thirty years up to 1999, Section 11 projects remained in place and continued to support schools, though the quantity and quality of the support changed over the years. The funding came from the Home Office, which imposed its own restrictions and limitations on projects. In 1999, Ethnic Minority Achievement Grants (EMAG) funding from the DfEE replaced Section 11 funding and much of the responsibility for this area of need was devolved to Local Authorities (LAs) and, in some cases, individual schools.

The report on the first major post-war research project on primary education was the Plowden Report: *Children and their Primary Schools* (Central Advisory Council for England, 1967). It advocated a child-centred approach, and this influenced teacher training and primary schools for a long time. The 1189-page report devoted six pages to the 'Children of Immigrants'. The ideology was very much one of assimilation, for example:

> It is absolutely essential to overcome the language barrier. This is less serious for the child entering the infant school. He [*sic*] rapidly acquires, both in the classroom and outside, a good command of the relatively limited number of words, phrases and sentences in common use among the children. He can then learn to read with the rest, by normal methods. (p71)

Several years after Plowden, the Bullock Report, *A Language for Life* (DES, 1975) was a major and influential statement about language in education in Britain. It located 'language' at the very heart of the curriculum, identifying and addressing the implications by arguing that all teachers – regardless of the subject or lesson taught – were first and foremost teachers of language. The 609-page report devoted twelve pages to 'Children of overseas origin', and the following, often quoted, paragraph sums up some of its dispositions in terms of ethnic minority children, making overt links – for the first time in a policy document in Britain – from language to culture and identity:

> Para: 20.5: Immigrant children's attainment in tests and school in general is related not only to language but to several other issues, particularly those of cultural identity and cultural knowledge. No child should be expected to cast off the language and culture of the home as he [*sic*] crosses the school threshold, nor to live and act as though school and home represent two totally separate and different cultures which have to be kept firmly apart. The curriculum should reflect many elements of that part of life which a child lives outside the school. (DES, 1975:286)

Around the same time as Bullock, language policies mediated by the European Union were attempting to respond to the growing phenomenon of economic migrancy. According to the (ECC) directive *The Children of Migrant Workers* (European Communities Council 1977), the

> ... host country must offer reception teaching. These educational measures for the reception include, in particular, tuition in the language or in one of the official languages of the host country adapted to the specific needs of foreign children. The host state is also under obligation to provide for the basic and further training of teachers who will take charge of the education of immigrant worker's children. Lastly, this Directive calls on the host states to take appropriate measures in co-operation with the states of origin, to promote the teaching of migrant's language and culture of origin. Such teaching should be co-ordinated with the work at school, that is, to be harmonised with the school curricula. (EEC, 1977:52)

In the light of this, two important projects were set up, funded by the DES, to explore multilingualism in Britain. The Mother Tongue and English Teaching Project (MOTET) in Bradford and Keighley is reported in Fitzpatrick (1987) and the other, the Linguistic Minorities Project, uncovered valuable information in different cities (Linguistic Minorities Project, 1985). Both have contributed to our knowledge about multilingualism and its potential for learning.

But such positive initiatives were developing in Britain within a wider social context of unrest and uncertainty about the needs of particular groups. Because of concerns felt by many teachers about meeting the needs of pupils from the Caribbean and also from their parents who felt strongly that the distinctive needs of their children were misunderstood, the government set up an enquiry to investigate West Indian children's perceived underachievement in school. The interim (Rampton) report appeared in 1981 (DES, 1981). The final report *Education for All* (the Swann Report) was published by the DES in 1985. Presenting evidence from School Leavers' Surveys, Swann showed that there were fundamental differences between English children's experiences of school and those of other ethnic groups. It revealed that, in statistical terms, many such groups seriously underachieved, West Indian and Bangladeshi heritage children in particular. But no single cause of underachievement was identified – ethnic group was only one factor together with social class, prejudice, racism, socio-economic background and so on. Swann offered no solution other than the requirement that all LAs and schools should generate their own multicultural education policies. A significant recommendation in terms of multilingualism was that communities, rather than primary or secondary schools, be responsible for teaching their own heritage languages. Most LAs took this as support for policies which totally separated the so-called 'community' languages from mainstream class-rooms.

The Swann Report has had long term but perhaps unforeseen effects on the ways that multilingualism is viewed in the wider British society (Conteh, 2006a). As the next section shows, it heralded a long process of mono-lingualising within the curriculum as a whole. It can be argued that it was also a key element of the general monolingualising ideology which still prevails in British politics. This trend is illustrated by Blackledge (2004) in his analysis of political speeches related to the 'Bradford riots' of 2001 and encapsulated in the now infamous quote from David Blunkett who, speaking as Home Secretary and former Secretary for Education about the riots in 2002, said:

> I have never said, or implied, that lack of fluency in English was in any way directly responsible for the disturbances in Bradford, Burnley and Oldham in the summer of 2001. However, speaking English enables parents to converse with their children in English, as well as in their historic mother tongue, at home and to participate in wider modern culture. It helps overcome the schizophrenia which bedevils generational relationships. In as many as 30% of Asian British households, according to the recent citizenship survey, English is not spoken at home. But let us be clear that lack of English fluency did not cause the riots. (Blunkett, 2002:77)

An inexcusable lack of awareness and understanding by a key political figure about the true picture of multilingualism in many British cities underpins this statement. The educational implications echo through all the chapters in this book.

1.3 *Multilingualism and the curriculum*

The Kingman Report (DES, 1988) was the first official statement about the proposed content of the putative National Curriculum for schools. Prior to 1988, schools in England and Wales had been able to devise their own curricula. Whereas the Plowden Report had placed the child at the centre of teaching and learning, and the Bullock Report had emphasised the language, the Kingman Report began from the forms of language and assessment. It presented a model of language teaching which it expected to cascade to schools. With its preoccupation with the role of grammar and assessment issues, such as what the child should know about English language at the age of 7, 11, 14 and 16 (the norm being the monolingual, native English-speaking child), it did not address the situation experienced by many British children who were learning English as their new or additional language.

The National Curriculum, with its new hierarchy of subjects, was introduced in 1989 and implemented in the early 1990s. Almost immediately, it was criticised by teachers as being both unmanageable and too narrow in its focus. It was revised in 1992 and again in 1995 when a so-called 'slimmed down' version was introduced. A final revision in 1999 gave us the 'Curriculum 2000' (DfEE, 1999a), but by then there had been other massive changes in the curriculum, particularly in primary schools, as we shall see. Throughout these revisions of the curriculum, both the structure and much of the content have remained the same, irrespective of the government that has completed the revision. Unlike its predecessors, however, the new Curriculum 2000 (DfEE, 1999a) makes its values explicit. The principles of inclusion (pp31-38), highlighting the needs of SEN, traveller and EAL pupils, were established. There are clear statements about so-called 'EAL' children:

> Pupils for whom English is an additional language have diverse needs in terms of support necessary in English language learning. Planning should take account of such factors as the pupil's age, length of time in this country, previous educational experiences and skills in other languages. ... Examples for developing spoken and written English ... **where appropriate**, encouraging pupils to transfer their knowledge and skills and understanding of one language to another, pointing out similarities and differences between languages ... building **on pupils' experiences of language at home** and in the wider community, so that their developing uses of English and other languages support one another. (DfEE, 1999a:37, emphasis added).

These statements have the potential for legitimising the use of community languages in English lessons. For the first time since the National Curriculum was devised, the school curriculum acknowledged the need to *build on* home languages. This can be interpreted positively to mean that other languages are now to be used throughout the child's school life and not just within the early stages of learning English and for transitional purposes. But in this potentially positive context, the words 'where appropriate' are a jarring, uncomfortable insertion which immediately begs the question: when is the use of a home language inappropriate?

When New Labour came to power in 1997, policy development followed very closely the agenda set by the Conservative government of the 1980s and 1990s. The overriding aim was to raise standards in literacy and numeracy. The National Literacy Strategy (DfEE, 1998) was published and implemented in 1998 and a daily Literacy Hour was introduced in English and Welsh primary schools. Whole class teaching and ability groups became the norm. Yearly and termly learning objectives were prescribed. The goal was that by 2002 at least

80% of 11 year olds (Year Six pupils) would achieve Level Four in English in KS2 national tests (formerly SATs). This did not happen, but the emphasis on performance had an inevitable impact on how bilingual children and their learning was perceived. Indeed, at first, any reference whatsoever to multi-lingualism was conspicuously absent from the widely distributed National Literacy Strategy file. In 1999, Section Four was belatedly published. This section specified support for SEN and EAL learners and was sent to schools several months after the initial framework had become established, clearly demonstrating the tagged-on, marginal status of these concerns in official dis-courses. It is also noticeable that EAL concerns were generally grouped to-gether with SEN issues, thus amplifying the deficit view of bilingualism.

The government continued to develop further its literacy initiatives, such as Additional, Early and Further Literacy Support (for a full list of initiatives, see DfES, 2003a). They shifted the role of classroom assistants to Learning Sup-port Assistants and Teaching Assistants, who were trained to deliver these support literacy packages. Grammar became an accepted part of literacy teaching and top-up lessons, booster classes and Easter schools were esta-blished. In fact, between 1998-2003, the Department for Education and Skills prepared 63 separate publications which aimed to raise standards in primary literacy and numeracy, 33 of them comprising training materials of different kinds. Additionally, there were eighteen supporting videos and twelve separate web-based packages. None of these centred on bilingual learners, nor did they consider their particular strengths or difficulties in relation to whole-class contexts. Instead an additional separate package for supporting EAL pupils was developed in 1999 (DfEE, 1999b), followed by the introduc-tion of new arrangements for funding provision for helping to raise the achievements of ethnic minority pupils (DfES, 2002a).

With the new century, a new dimension is being added to language in pri-mary schools. Based on recommendations from the National Languages Steering Group formed after Nuffield Languages Inquiry, the National Lan-guages Strategy (DfES, 2002b) aims to enable *all* primary school children to learn another language:

> Our vision is clear – we must provide an opportunity for early language learning to harness children's learning potential and enthusiasm, we must provide high quality teaching and learning opportunities to equip our young people with the skills they need to access opportunities for lifelong language learning; we must recognise lan-guage skills as central to breaking barriers both within this country and between our nation and others. (DfES, 2002b:4)

But, as Conteh demonstrates in Chapter Seven, the obvious links between so-called 'community' and 'modern foreign' languages are not made in this initiative, nor in the recently introduced framework for languages at Key Stage Two (DfES, 2005a).

In primary education more widely, several recent policy documents support the move to a more flexible and creative approach to teaching and learning. Together, these can be seen to provide spaces to develop ways to nurture and promote multilingualism in primary classrooms and links with communities, so perhaps we can dare to be cautiously optimistic about the future of multi-lingualism in the mainstream. For example, *Excellence and Enjoyment: A Strategy for Primary Schools* (DfES, 2003b), part of the Primary National Strategy (which includes the National Literacy and Numeracy Strategies), specifies:

> Good primary schools know that working with parents and the community and thinking beyond the normal school day is vital to helping children get the best from their learning. ... As well as working closely with parents, primary schools must be closely linked to their communities. They are and should be a community resource; and they can also benefit from those around them ... Many make use of skilled adults from the local community – from volunteers, to local businesses who read with children, to local police officers or fire fighters who give talks and demonstrate what they do. ... Interchange between schools and the community benefits every-one and helps local people to see the value in their school. (DfES, 2003b:51)

Similarly, the *Every Child Matters* (DfES, 2003c) agenda promotes an inte-grated, multidisciplinary approach to education and care of all children and young people (from birth to 19 years):

> Section 10 of the Children Act 2004 places duty on local authorities and their res-pective partners ... to co-operate to improve children and young people's well being. It also specifies that co-operation should extend to other bodies that are involved with delivering services to children and young people – a description that includes voluntary and community organisations.

The *Aiming High* initiative through several useful publications, such as *Aim-ing High; Raising Attainment for Minority Ethnic Pupils* (DfES, 2003d), offers hopeful messages for the future of links between community and main-stream schooling in Britain:

> 2.36 Successful schools reach out to communities. They often make premises available for community use, which can build bridges and develop dialogue. Many pupils have also benefited greatly from out-of-hours learning in community-run initiatives such as supplementary schools.' (DfES, 2003d:n.p.)

Finally, a recent set of teaching and background materials has been developed from the PNS/EAL pilot project (NALDIC, 2004) and disseminated as part of the *Excellence and Enjoyment* strategy. Thus, it is aimed at both literacy and EAL consultants and offers many hopeful signs in the development of what could be described as bilingual pedagogies in primary schools (DfES, 2006).

2. *Community responses and actions*

As noted in the previous section, minority ethnic communities in Britain have largely been left to themselves to maintain their languages. Although the Bullock Report (DES, 1975) stated that children should not be expected to leave their languages and cultures at home once they enter the school gates, and EEC directives have made reference to promoting the teaching of migrants' language and culture of origin, formal support for minority ethnic languages has not been forthcoming. Perhaps the clearest statement, as noted above, is to be found in the Swann Report, which noted that cultural and linguistic maintenance was beyond the remit of mainstream education and, instead, is 'best achieved within the ethnic minority communities themselves' (DES, 1985:406).

In fact, minority ethnic communities have, for many years, been involved in setting up 'after hours' schools in order to promote their cultures and languages although little was known about such schools outside the communities themselves. This type of education has been referred to by many different terms, such as complementary, community, supplementary, or heritage language education, and we return to a discussion of this terminology later in this chapter.

Brief historical accounts of after hours education appear in McLean (1985) and Tomlinson (1984), who refer to the challenge such education provides to state education in Britain. Similarly, Edwards (2001) and the Linguistic Minorities Project (1985), provide some information on the increase in after hours education from the seventies onwards. In a more recent contribution, Li Wei (2006) looks at the past, present and future of this form of education.

On a more practical level, the Resource Unit for Supplementary and Mother Tongue Schools (www.continyou.org.uk) has published a potentially useful *Directory of Supplementary and Mother-Tongue Classes 1999-2000* (Kempadoo and Abdelrazak, 1999), as well as guidelines for improving such schools (Abdelrazak, 2001). According to the website, the Resource Unit offers advice to a network of over 800 schools in the UK.

Many of the early schools were set up by African-Caribbean communities as they were dissatisfied about the type of education their children were receiving in the state sector. According to Chevannes and Reeves (1987:159):

> ... the existence of the black voluntary school is predicated on the black population's unsatisfactory experience and appraisal of British education – an experience composed of all the classical ingredients of social alienation: powerlessness, meaninglessness, social isolation and self-estrangement.

A considerable amount of work has been carried out on black supplementary schools by, for example, Mirza and Reay (2000) and Reay and Mirza (2001). Their work shows how such schools provide safe spaces for alternative discourses from dominant mainstream positions, what they have referred to as 'spaces and places of black educational desire' (Mirza and Reay, 2000:521). Unfortunately, we are unable to include an account of these alternative discourses, or stories, in Black supplementary schools in this volume. It is, however, recognised that there is a significant story to tell. In the important work which Mirza and Reay carried out, they note how:

> ... the discursive constructions of community and blackness ... contribute to the formation of collective black identities which work against the hegemony of whiteness and individualism within wider society. (2000:525)

There are important resonances here with stories told in the other chapters in this volume.

It would appear that most schools that were set up in the latter part of the last century were for the purposes of cultural and linguistic maintenance. The view of Verma *et al* (1994:12) is that the main function of community language education is to support 'cultural and religious identity in the face of the threat of cultural assimilation'. Hall *et al* (2002) take this further, suggesting that such schools correct the rather 'subtractive' approach to learning language in the mainstream sector. According to Hall *et al*, 'mainstream schooling at best neglects, and at worst denies cultural and linguistic diversity to such an extent that communities mount their own provision at considerable cost to themselves' (Hall *et al*, 2002:415). They also make the salient point that this form of education has received little attention in the literature and remains under theorised, a point with which we agree.

However, there are signs that after hours learning is beginning to get the attention it deserves. Li Wei (1993) has reported on Chinese schools in Newcastle and their role in the maintenance of the language. In another study on the Chinese community, Wu (2006) explores language choice and Chinese cultures of learning in Chinese schools. Khan and Kabir (1999) have studied Bengali teaching to Bangladeshi children in Swansea, and Arthur (2003) explores language and literacy learning among the Somali community in Liverpool. These and other studies, some of which are made reference to in the paper by Martin *et al* in this volume, have helped in our understanding of what goes on in such schools, and allows us to theorise about the management of bilingualism, identity formation and the value-added nature of such schooling.

A recent report (Martin *et al*, 2004) indicates the importance of after hours education in several areas such as the management of bilingualism, the enhancement of learning and the ways in which schools widen the students' choices and uptake of identities. Tikly *et al* (DfES, 2002a) have linked the attendance at supplementary schools to increased attainment of pupils of African Caribbean heritage. Perhaps most significantly, the government has begun to recognise the potential value-added nature of complementary schooling, as the references to the *Aiming High* initiative in the previous section indicate.

3. *Theoretical and methodological frameworks*

The history of community based teaching and learning in Britain is inevitably and strongly influenced by national and international events as well as on-going social, political and economic trends. In many ways, the key to understanding the issues which they face lies in mapping the interplay between the local and the global. As Agar (2005:20) shows with his analogy of fractals, this is what will help us to see the 'structure of patterns at different levels of scale' or – to put it another way – Bateson's 'patterns that connect'. A wide range of disciplines, including sociology, history, cultural psychology (Cole, 1996), sociolinguistics, discourse studies and cultural studies, contributes to this understanding. In this section, we present an overview of some theoretical frameworks which can help explain the issues and indicate ways forward for research, policy development and practice in community schooling. It is presented in three main parts, which take us progressively deeper into the layers of interaction that surround the learning experiences of children in community based contexts. These are:

- The outer layer – understanding the system

- The intermediate layer – school ethos and classroom organisation

- The inner layer – conversations between teachers and learners.

At the heart of the whole discussion there needs to be a well theorised model of learning. This also needs to take account of the global and the local – the broader social, cultural and political factors which impact on learning, as well as the detailed substance of particular classroom interactions where learning is successfully (or otherwise) negotiated. It needs to link language, culture and identity, all crucial factors in individual learners' (and teachers') success. It needs to include a concept of power which recognises that all players in the game of learning are active and purposive, though with unequal access to the most powerful discourses. As Gee (2005:2) argues, language can never be considered a politically neutral phenomenon – power is 'part and parcel of using language'. As he goes on to stress, this idea adds weight to the argument that we need to 'engage with the details' of interaction in order to understand the bigger picture.

Vygotskyan sociocultural theories (Lantolf, 2000) are now a familiar element in descriptions and explanations of language learning. Close examination of classroom dialogues shows how the conversations between teachers and pupils are important sites for the co-construction of knowledge and the nego-tiation of pupils' chances for success. They reveal how teachers can construct affordances (van Lier, 2000) for supporting their pupils' thinking and learn-ing. Lantolf conceptualises the familiar Vygotskyan notion of the ZPD as:

> ...the collaborative construction of opportunities ... for individuals to develop their mental abilities (2000:17)

However, as Maybin (2003:3-4) argues, the ZPD is often constructed in educa-tional research in England as more closely related to language than to culture and identity. She suggests that, in research into classroom interaction, too strong a focus on only the linguistic features of talk can take us away from Vykotsky's original conception of the ZPD as 'a site of socialisation as well as conceptual development' (p3). Such a view resonates with the ideas of cul-tural psychologists such as Cole (1985, 1996), who recognise the ways in which both teachers and learners mediate experiences in classrooms through the lenses of their personal and cultural histories. Cummins (2001:2) argues that, through such negotiations, if the 'deep structure of relationships be-tween educators and culturally diverse students' (p136) is oriented towards 'empowerment' rather than reproducing the 'coercive relations of power operating in the wider society', the culture of the classroom can be trans-formed and genuine equality of opportunity can become a possibility.

3.1 *The outer layer – understanding the system*

As Bruner (1996:28) reminds us, schools are always shaped by the 'external' culture of society as a whole, and in turn contribute to wider societal cultures. What happens within schools is always a mediation of the local and the global contexts which they inhabit and a reflection of the patterns of power and inequality in these wider contexts. As Tollefson (1995:2) argues, language policies are both 'an outcome of power struggles and an arena for those struggles'. As we have seen in Section One, the rhetoric of equality of opportunity shines through many policy documents related to language in education, but at the same time they often serve to perpetuate long-established inequalities. In this section, we describe two theoretical frameworks, the first from anthropology and the second from sociology, which can help explain this and also illuminate some of the systemic issues which have led to the development of community based learning in Britain.

In order to understand fully 'the situatedness of education in the society at large' and the ways in which global concerns play out in the particular interactions between teachers and learners, Bruner (1996) stresses the need for a broad 'anthropology of education', as well as detailed ethnographies of individual classrooms. But it needs to be anthropology with a critical stance. Ogbu's (1981) 'multilevel approach' to school ethnography meets these requirements. Through it, he illustrates how 'forces originating in other settings' influence classroom teaching and learning. Linked to this, Bourdieu's concepts of habitus, field and capital help to reveal the complex reasons why certain groups of pupils fail in school and the problems attached to concluding that these reasons reside solely within individual pupils themselves. They enable us to see the need to take account of pupils' experiences in a wide range of contexts in order to understand their learning strengths and needs.

Ogbu traces the history of school ethnographies in the USA from the 1960s, arguing that those studies which focus on finding explanations for 'minority school failure' often depend heavily on sociolinguistic frameworks. They tend to conclude that the problems are caused by miscommunications between teachers and pupils within classrooms, and so the solutions must lie in changing classroom practices. But, as Ogbu points out, this does not provide an explanation for many thorny issues, such as the ways that success or failure are experienced differently by different ethnic groups. For this, he argues, we need to search for explanations outside the classroom and the school. His 'multilevel' or 'cultural ecological' approach to a 'more complete ethnography' (pp14-15) is based on four underlying assumptions:

1. Education is linked in important ways with economics and economic opportunities in society.

2. It is important to study the history of these economic links.

3. Participants behave in ways which are influenced by their models of social reality.

4. A full ethnography needs to study the societal and historical forces which have influenced schools.

Through his studies of African American communities in California, Ogbu was able to reveal how failure in mainstream school was almost a foregone conclusion for these black pupils because of a complex combination of economic disadvantage, low teacher expectation (not just of the individual pupils, but of their families) and a growing culture of mistrust built up over generations – in this way, their failure was systemic, not an outcome of individual deficit.

Carrington and Luke (1997) use Bourdieu's well known sociological model as an analytic tool to critique educational and social practices such as literacy teaching. They call the 'plausibility structures' built up to explain school success 'folk theories', and offer another one – that 'literacy ... has become equated with the advancement and overall well being of individuals, communities and entire societies' (p97). They go on to show how such a simplistic notion with its narrow model of what constitutes literacy has been called into question by the growing body of research and writing on 'literacies' as social practices. Bourdieu argues that 'literacies may constitute forms of cultural capital which, in synergistic combination with other forms of capital, may command value in some social contexts.' (Carrington and Luke, 1997:104). From this perspective, it can be argued that mainstream schools construct 'highly specific literate practices' which 'may not yield the only significant discourses and practices which are required by individuals ...' (p105). Thus, a child entering mainstream school in Britain who is fluent in Urdu may accrue less cultural capital for her bilingualism than a child fluent in French or Spanish, and so have less scope to benefit from the cognitive advantages which her bilingualism may afford her. She may be developing her literacy in Urdu in a community based context (and gaining cultural capital for doing so there) but under the current policy regime in Britain this is likely to remain hidden from her mainstream teachers, and so be of limited value to her success in this particular context.

Carrington and Luke's conclusions in many ways echo those of Ogbu. In different ways, their work reveals how individual learners' successes and failures are intimately bound up with decisions made about wider educational systems and policies, over which they usually have no control. They show the importance of understanding the full range of learning and other social experiences which impinge on what happens in classrooms, and offer two valuable theoretical and methodological tools – multilevel ethnography and Bourdieu's sociological analysis – to help us to do so. With tools such as these, we can begin to unpick the ways in which the wider social and political system in Britain has shaped the development of community based learning, and how future development can be guided and enhanced.

3.2 *The intermediate layer – school ethos and classroom organisation*

The ecological metaphor remains appropriate as we move to the intermediate layer, that of the school and within it, the classroom. Ecological perspectives are not currently common in the study of language in classrooms in Britain. The strength of such an approach for the study of multilingual classrooms and community based learning lies in the way it reveals 'the complex inter-relationships, interactions and ideologies within such classrooms' (Creese and Martin, 2003:161). Classroom ecologies can be 'proactive in pulling apart perceived natural language orders ...' (p164), for example in revealing the tensions between ideologies embodied in national policy and the ways in which they are mediated in schools and classrooms. The National Curriculum ideology of 'diversity and inclusion' is a powerful example of a policy which reveals its inherent contradictions when examined from an ecological perspective. It is historically constructed on a model of equality which is often naturalised as sameness. In terms of language diversity in mainstream primary classrooms, it creates a conundrum in many ways for most (monolingual) teachers. For example, they are invited to 'celebrate' the diversity represented by their pupils, but must measure their success only in terms of their attainment in English.

Work by Angel Lin (1999) in classrooms in Hong Kong combines an ecological perspective with Bourdieu's framework to show the ways that students' attitudes towards learning English are strongly influenced by their perceived relationships with their teachers, and the ways they position themselves in relation to the values placed on proficiency in English in the wider society. Using Bourdieu's notions of 'cultural capital' and 'habitus', that is, the 'language use, skills, and orientations, attitudes, dispositions, and schemes of perception that children are endowed with by virtue of socialisation in their families and communities' (Lin, 1999:407), Lin explores the compatibility of what students bring with them into the English language classroom, and what the lesson required of them. She refers to the dilemmas faced by teachers and students in classrooms situated in different socio-economic areas of Hong Kong, and the 'creative discursive strategies' they develop to face up to them.

In one classroom, lessons reinforced what the students brought with them (their 'habitus') into the school. In some classrooms, what the students brought with them was incompatible with what the English lesson required, leading them to misbehave and resist the teacher's attempts to teach in English. However, in another classroom, Lin reports how the teacher, through her 'discursive, creative agency' managed to transform the attitudes and experiences of the students so that meaningful learning took place. This she did by the strategic use of the students' first language (Cantonese) in a reading lesson in order to 'intertwine an interesting story focus and a language learning focus' (Lin, 1999:409).

3.3 *The inner layer – conversations between teachers and learners*

At the heart of our understanding of community based learning contexts are the classroom conversations among teachers, other adults and learners. Researchers working in multilingual classrooms have developed a range of theoretical and analytic frameworks to examine the fine grained detail of these interactions. In different ways, they show emphatically how classroom conversations are more than just neutral conduits for the transmission of knowledge. They are also the medium for the social and cultural processes which are crucial for negotiating learners' and teachers' identities and so for success. Such frameworks share the quality of being emergent; rather than having pre-defined categories, the analyst generates categories from within the data. In order to do this with confidence, she/he needs both insider knowledge of the contexts being studied and outsider knowledge of the layers which surround them.

Different frameworks pay attention to different aspects of discourse. Conversation analysis from a sociological perspective (Drew, 1990), for example, focuses on turn taking and is helpful in revealing the ways participants co-construct meanings. Narrative analysis (Gee, 1985, 1991) identifies patterns of organisation in spoken texts and provides a model for examining an individual participant's sense making in a particular context. Of particular relevance to multilingual classrooms are frameworks for analysing codeswitching (Mercer, 2001), which contribute to our growing awareness of its value as a classroom strategy. Fairclough's (2003) critical discourse analysis is a powerful tool to reveal how language contributes to the domination of some people by others and how such domination becomes naturalised in specific contexts. For example, a bilingual classroom assistant may have far deeper knowledge of the language and cultural backgrounds of the pupils she is working with than the class teacher, but her skills and knowledge are marginalised because of her position in the classroom hierarchy. Recent research has also investigated biliteracy (Datta, 2001) or what has been termed simultaneous literacies (Kenner, 2000a; Gregory *et al*, 2004; Robertson, 2006) and is beginning to develop frameworks for analysing the ways children mediate their experiences of literacies in different languages and different scripts.

Teacher talk is also an important field of study. Often, in multilingual learning contexts, teachers do not share the language and cultural backgrounds of their pupils. A wide range of linguistic-ethnographic studies explore the issues which arise (eg Cazden *et al*, 1972; Trueba *et al*, 1981; Philips, 1983; Heath, 1983; Nieto, 1999). This work has contributed to the development of models of culturally relevant pedagogy, such as that synthesised by Osborne (1996). Such research has been much more common in the USA and Australia than in Britain, but Callender's (1997) study of teachers and pupils from African-Caribbean backgrounds in London contributes to our understanding of the ways in which culture plays out in interactions between teachers and pupils in schools. She shows how black teachers effectively weave cultural practices, such as patterns of language use, into their discourses and, in this way, signal inclusion and empowerment to their pupils, rather than the more common messages of exclusion and alienation. Other studies of bilingual teachers in British contexts (eg Creese, 2005; Conteh, 2007) are beginning to show the need for frameworks which recognise the diversity of interaction in multilingual classrooms and the implications for teacher education, policy and practice.

4. *Statement on terminology and presentation*
There are a plethora of terms used to describe community learning contexts, the teachers and learners who inhabit them and the languages which are mediated. Our aim here is not to analyse the terminology in detail but to raise questions about the powerful ideological messages embedded in particular terms. As far as the sites of out of hours learning are concerned, the most commonly used terms are 'supplementary' and 'complementary' schooling, both of which, as Robertson (2005) has pointed out, suggest an 'add-on' to

'mainstream' learning – itself a contested term within this discussion. Other terms used, which include 'community language schools' and 'heritage schools', are not neutral and do not encompass everything the schools do. They can be seen to suggest that the languages themselves are of a lower status and more limited function than English.

In terms of the teachers and pupils, a key issue of terminology is – as referred to in the National Census (2001) – the question of ethnic categories. The fifteen listed in the 2001 census are clearly contestable. But the question remains about which terms are recognisably inclusive and descriptive. For example, the term most commonly used in policy by the TDA (the Training and Development Agency for Teachers, the government-sponsored agency for teacher training and development in England) 'minority ethnic' teachers implies difference and even deficit as compared with the majority. As discussed in Conteh (pp124-125 in this volume) there need to be terms which reflect the potential benefits which such teachers can bring to classroom contexts.

Debates about language terminology have gone on for several years (Rampton *et al*, 1997). Perhaps the key issue for the stories told in this book is that we need terms which encapsulate the simultaneity and flexibility of language use in multilingual communities; which reflect that codeswitching, mixing and similar practices are normal and natural for bilingual and multilingual speakers, as can be seen in the conversations between teachers and learners in this book. Terms such as 'EAL' 'ESL' 'first language' and so on all tend to indicate a model of sequentially adding on one language to another, whereas, as the examples in the chapters show, the reality is more a case of 'syncretism' (Gregory *et al*, 2004) or the enrichment of one language through another.

At this stage in these debates, we believe that it is important not to forestall discussion by being prescriptive about choice of terms. For this reason, we have made the decision not to standardise the use of terminology throughout the chapters of this book. The authors of each chapter have chosen the terms which they believe best reflect their particular contexts and frameworks. This includes the transliterative English spellings of words from other languages, such as Gujerati/Gujurati. With these, we have followed the conventions used by each author, as well as the communities themselves in these contexts, and so spellings may vary in different chapters. In using words from different languages, our preference would be – following Edwards (2005:24) – 'to show that minority languages are in fact a normal part of life' and not to use italics. But, in the transcripts of the conversations, we believe it is important to highlight the multilingual aspect of the unfolding stories, and italics is an effective way of doing this. So, in order to be consistent and to comply with the publisher's house style, we have italicised words from different languages throughout the book. As with the terminology, we decided not to standardise the presentation of the transcripts and other data, and have maintained the individual authors' transcription conventions.

5. *Overview of the volume*

The volume consists of this introductory chapter and seven further chapters, which provide particular cases of multilingual learning stories in schools and communities in Britain. The final chapter, by Jill Bourne, draws together the themes which emerge in the volume and identifies possibilities for the future.

Chapter Two, *Learning in Three Languages in Home and Community* by Raymonde Sneddon, focuses on children in a Gujerati Muslim community in north east London. It relates how these children live their daily lives in three languages. In her ethnographic study, Sneddon uses interviews, observations, recordings and questionnaires in order to explore the children's use of Gujerati, Urdu and English in the school, the home and the community classes. Sneddon reports on the complex negotiations of language that go on in the children's homes, in the school and in the wider community. By the term 'community' she includes the classes that the children attend. She makes the point that, although schools nowadays are aware of the language repertoire of the children, little use is made of their linguistic and literacy knowledge, as well as the complex metalinguistic skills they have learned in their community classes. In the conclusion to her study, Sneddon urges for closer collaboration between mainstream schools, complementary schools and families.

Chapter Three, *The Story of Bilingual Children Learning to Read* by Leena Helavaara Robertson, tells the story of five bilingual children, of British Pakistani background, who are learning to read. These children attend the Reception class in their local school and learn to read English in a daily one-hour literacy lesson. Around the time when they move on to their Year One class, they also begin to attend daily Qur'anic literacy lessons at the local mosque and at home, where they learn to read in classical Arabic. Some months later, a local peripatetic EMAG teacher begins weekly lunchtime Urdu lessons at the children's school. The five children learn to read in three different languages (they speak a fourth one, Pahari, at home). Robertson reports on the teachers' grouping arrangements and shows how children's groups reveal different types of expectations and strikingly different views of children as learners.

Chapter Four by Yangguang Chen is entitled *Contributing to Success: Chinese parents and the community school*. As the title suggests, the major thrust of the story told in this chapter is 'success', and the reasons why many Chinese learners in the school system in Britain are high achievers. The paper considers the role of parents in their children's education as well as the role of the community language schools which the children attend. Chen focuses on the attitudes to education of two newly arrived families, as well as the families of five children who have lived in Britain for more than three years. Using interviews, Chen explores the views of family members. She concludes that Chinese community language schools play an important role in children's educational success and, in addition, they are significant in that they provide a bridge between the parent and children generations and between two languages and cultures.

In Chapter Five, *Learning Portuguese: a tale of two worlds*, Olga Barradas tells the story of children attending Portuguese language and culture classes in Lambeth, a socio-economically poor area of south London. At the outset, Barradas provides extensive discussion on the history of after hours Portuguese learning/teaching in Britain and she goes on to relate several important issues in the organisation and running of this form of education. Among the factors considered by Barradas are educational achievement and the development of both cultural and learner identity, the increasing importance of e-learning and the Primary Languages Strategy. A feature of this chapter are the insights from participants in the study which occur throughout the chapter.

In Chapter Six, Peter Martin, Arvind Bhatt, Nirmala Bhojani and Angela Creese tell *Multilingual Learning Stories in Two Gujarati Complementary Schools in Leicester*. This chapter emerges from a year long study of complementary schools in Leicester. The contribution shows how the two schools in the study challenge the monolingual ethos which generally exists in Britain. Using interviews with students and teachers and recordings of classroom observation, the study demonstrates how use of two languages is the norm in the schools, and how this goes beyond the celebration of language, but is rather a spontaneous educational experience which is both inclusive and empowering. At the same time, the use of more than one language challenges the ideologies which exist in the wider environment and reaffirms the importance of Gujarati in relation to different types of identities.

In Chapter Seven, *Culture, Languages and Learning: mediating a bilingual approach in complementary Saturday classes*, Jean Conteh describes the work of teachers in a complementary class in the city of Bradford in northern England. The main aim of the classes described in this study is to help develop emergent bilingual children's knowledge of and confidence in their home and community languages as a means of raising their achievement in mainstream schooling. The teachers themselves are all British born bilinguals educated in schools in England in the 1970s and 1980s, so their experiences as pupils were directly influenced by the policies outlined in this introductory chapter. As qualified primary teachers, from their training and personal experiences, they have developed a vision of bilingual learning and teaching. The chapter reveals the significance of this for their professional identities as mainstream primary teachers.

The concluding chapter by Jill Bourne both contextualises the stories in the writer's personal experiences of language diversity in England over the past thirty years, and indicates how they link with global trends and themes in language education and research. In so doing, it raises important questions about the challenges and opportunities for all teachers in England as they work with increasingly diverse groups of learners. And it suggests the – as yet relatively unexplored – potential of multilingual pedagogies for contributing to the identities of those learners as they become both confident British citizens and members of global society.

Table One: Key Events in Policy

1963	Report *English for Immigrants* (DES)
1966	Local Government Act, Section 11
1967	Report *Children and their Primary Schools* – the Plowden Report (DES)
1974	Report *Educational Disadvantage and Educational Needs of Immigrants* (DES)
1975	Report *A Language for Life* – the Bullock Report (DES)
1977	European Communities Council's (ECC) directive *The Children of Migrant Workers* (European Communities Council)
1981	*Mother Tongue and English Teaching Project* (MOTET) (Rees and Fitzpatrick)
1981	*Linguistic Minorities Project* (Linguistic Minorities Project)
1981	*West Indian Children in Our Schools* – Rampton Report (DES)

1985   Education for All – Swann Report (DES)

1988   Report of the Committee of Inquiry into Teaching of English Language – Kingman Report

1988   Education Reform Act

1992   The National Curriculum

1995   National Curriculum revision

1997   Parliamentary election – New Labour wins a landslide victory

1998   Introduction of the National Literacy Strategy

1999   EAL support within the National Literacy Strategy – Section Four

1999   Ethnic Minority Achievement Grant (EMAG)

1999   New National Curriculum 2000 (DfEE)

2002   The National Languages Strategy *Languages for All: Languages for Life* – introduction of 'MFL' into primary classrooms (DfES)

2002   Speech by the Home Secretary, David Blunkett (Secretary for Education 1997-2001) – *Integration with Diversity*

2003   *Aiming High; Raising Attainment for Minority Ethnic Pupils* (DfES)

2003   *Excellence and Enjoyment: A Strategy for Primary Schools* (DfES)

2003   *Every Child Matters* (DfES)

2005   *KS2 Framework for Languages* (DfES)

2006   *Excellence and Enjoyment: Learning and Teaching for Bilingual Children in the Primary Years* (DfES)

2
Learning in Three Languages in Home and Community

Raymonde Sneddon

Introducing Rehana

'Well, it depends, sometimes I say *hathi* and sometimes I say *elephant,* because it came first into my head'.

Rehana is retelling the story of the Raja's Big Ears (Desai, 1989) in Gujerati. She is just a little nervous of the tape-recorder at first and mutters a couple of times under her breath 'how do you say...?' Then she gets into the flow: the story takes off, the dialogue is lively and the chants come in both English and Gujerati:

The raja's got big ears!
The raja's got big ears!
Who told you?
Who told you?

In the same way as story tellers of that age drive their stories along in English with *and then, and then,* Rehana links her narrative with *pachi, pachi.* A number of English words come into her story, as they came first into her head: *musical instruments, party, table, tambourine, secret.*

Rehana is 11 years old and was born in London. Her Gujerati has features of the Surti dialect that her family speak. She makes some mistakes: gender is a minefield for bilingual children who have become dominant in English, and Gujerati has three. In the language of the story there are some words that are unfamiliar in both her main languages, like *barber* (*hajam* in Gujerati): 'it's not a word I use in Gujerati, it's a story word; but I don't use it in English much either, I say *hair cutter* or *hairdresser*'.

'My Dad doesn't like us to speak English at home. He tells us off'. Both Rehana's parents were born and educated to secondary school level in India in Gujerati, Urdu, Hindi and English and they have literacy skills, in varying degrees, in all these languages. They are keen to pass on Gujerati, the main language of the family. Rehana learned English when she went to nursery. As well as hearing her read in English every day when she was younger, as the school recommended, Rehana's mother told her stories in Gujerati. Her father is heavily involved in the running of a centre that caters for the needs of the Gujerati and Urdu speaking community, so there are lots of documents in Gujerati and Urdu around the house and both languages are used regularly for reading and writing.

As a Muslim, Rehana goes to school very near home and attends the madressa (religious classes attached to the mosque) in a large, converted Victorian house in the same street. There are many opportunities for her to use Gujerati as well as English in most areas of her life: there are Gujerati children in her class at school, she attends a playcentre where all children are Gujerati/English bilinguals, she goes swimming regularly with her friends, many of whom are also Gujerati speakers. She uses all these opportunities, though how much Gujerati she speaks depends on the context.

At school and at the swimming pool she speaks a little Gujerati with her friends. At playcentre, she switches from Gujerati to English depending on what she is doing and who is she is with, but the balance there is more towards English. However, playing with friends at home she speaks Gujerati more than half the time and switches back and forward from one language to the other. At the Madressa she speaks mostly Gujerati to her friends and to her teacher, who is more confident in Gujerati than English, although this is mixed with words and phrases in English. She is learning Urdu at Madressa and speaks it a little at home. Her mother helps her every day with reading her religious books in Urdu.

Although her parents resolutely speak to her in Gujerati, like many bilingual children, she answers half of the time in English, in spite of Dad's telling off. She is a very fluent speaker of English, in which she can tell a wonderfully expressive version of the Raja's big ears, and she has achieved level four in English (the level expected of monolingual English speaking children) and level five (a higher than expected level) in maths in her Key Stage Two SATs, the tests for children in England at the end of primary school.

Introduction and context

Rehana's story is one of 36 that I explored as part of a study of children who live their daily lives in three languages in a Gujerati Muslim community in north east London. The children were aged three and a half to 11. Through interviews, observations, recordings and questionnaires, their experiences of learning literacy in Gujerati, Urdu and English were explored in school, in the home and in community classes. The children's use of their three languages was tracked through the three generations of their families and in many different areas of their daily lives in the community.

I originally encountered the community through my work as a teacher in a multilingual primary school in which they formed the largest language group. As a new teacher in the late 1970s with a background in linguistics, I became very interested in the many languages spoken at home by the children in my school. While the main focus of my work was to teach English as an additional language, my own experiences as a bilingual led me to build the use of children's home languages into the everyday life of the school. I was greatly supported and encouraged in this by the staff at the Inner London Education Authority's (ILEA) Centre for Urban Educational Studies and colleagues on the Language in the Multicultural Primary Classroom Project based at the Institute of Education in London.

Over the next few years, parents and older siblings had a major linguistic input into the school. Initially they came into the classroom to look at their own children's work, to write captions for photos, and text in the family language for a child's book. Some came to tell stories in home languages, initially to groups, then to the whole class; they made story tapes and story posters, bilingual books with their own children about personal experiences, and invented games that encouraged children to share their languages with each other. Parents and children helped us to pilot multiscript word processing software that was being developed specifically for use by pupils and teachers in London schools (Sneddon, 1998). A group of mothers went together to a multilingual bookshop to choose books for the school library.

Children told me about the community classes that they attended and I was invited to visit Saturday schools in which they learned Punjabi, Turkish and Bengali. The ILEA Mother Tongue teaching service were persuaded to provide a part time teacher of Gujerati, the language with the largest number of speakers in the school, to teach all children who wished to attend, in school time. We set up a Saturday Bengali school on school premises, managed by the parents, who had requested it for their children.

As a teacher at a time when primary French was still being taught and knowledge of European languages was valued, I was aware of the very different status accorded to the bilingualism of the children I taught. While some of my colleagues were positive about encouraging children to use their first languages and impressed with their knowledge and skills, others worried that maintaining these languages would confuse children like Rehana and damage their educational opportunities. When I started investigating research on bilingualism, I found these contradictory attitudes reflected in the literature reviewed by Hamers and Blanc (1989) and Baker (2001). The theoretical model developed by Cummins (1984) addressed these issues and offered explanations for apparently contradictory research results. The Common Underlying Proficiency (Cummins, 1984) suggests that concepts and skills developed in one language transfer readily to another. The circumstances in which children learn two or more languages can significantly affect whether or not they develop as *additive bilinguals*: adding a second language to their first and becoming confident users of two languages in a wide range of situations, or as *subtractive bilinguals*: losing the use of their first language as they acquire their second.

According to the model, which type of bilingual the children become depends on whether they have acquired a strong level of concept development and proficiency in their first language when they encounter their second. Children who have access to education in their first language acquire their second language with greater ease and proficiency. Studies with balanced bilinguals (Peal and Lambert, 1962) and evaluations of bilingual education programmes have shown the intellectual benefits derived from additive bilingualism (Thomas and Collier, 1997; Cummins, 2001).

Bilingual education is not on offer in the mainstream system for speakers of community languages in England and the low value put on skills in these languages suggested that the children in my school were likely to become subtractive bilinguals. Cummins' empowerment model (2001) provided the rationale for valuing community languages within the school, encouraging attendance at mother tongue schools (as we called them then), and providing first language teaching on the premises whenever possible.

Common patterns of European bilingualism (such as my own, in French and English) fit in very nicely with the Cummins model: if children speak two standard European languages and have opportunities for education in the language they speak in the home (give or take some differences in regional and social dialects); they are very likely to become additive bilinguals, speaking languages that have high status in the wider community. By contrast, in multilingual countries the world over, many people speak languages that are not written or not available in education. Different languages are generally used for different purposes and it is a common experience for children to be educated in a language or language variety that is very different from the one that is spoken in their home.

When I set out to study language use and literacy practices in the Gujerati community, the Cummins' model was at the heart of my hypotheses. I was looking for evidence of what impact support in the language and literacy of the home might have on children's lives and, eventually, on their achievement in school.

The reality of what I found proved to be far more complex than I had anticipated, as the following will demonstrate.

Language and literacy in multilingual families

The study described here focused on a three generation community of Gujerati speaking Indian Muslims who started settling in north east London in the late 1960s. They came from the district of Surat in Gujerat, many of them from the same village, Bardoli. Ties of kinship and friendship are strong and the community have remained close. They come from primarily rural backgrounds and have a lower socio-economic profile than Gujerati communities in the west of London (Linguistic Minorities Project, 1985; Dave, 1991), who are primarily Hindus with professional backgrounds, many of whom came to London from Kenya. Elders of the community described the economic and social challenges which they experienced on arrival. In the face of racism and discrimination, the community organised itself. At the present time, a mosque and community centre occupying three large adjacent houses are witness to the community's concern to provide facilities for their members. As practising Muslims, the families wanted their children to attend daily religious instruction after school in the madressa which is part of the mosque. Many live within walking distance of the mosque. The community centre, founded in 1980, famously provides cradle-to-grave services for the whole community including classes, youth and sports activities and a crèche. Local knowledge suggested to me that this community centre played an important part in children's lives.

The community which I studied speak a dialect of Gujerati. Those who have been educated in India, like Rehana's parents, were educated in the standard variety and were also literate in Urdu and other languages such as Hindi or

Arabic. Urdu is the more prestigious language used by Muslims in India: it is the language of power, of literature and of the quality press. It has much greater status than the regional language of Gujerati. Crucially, it is the language of religious instruction, through which the Qur'an is interpreted. While Gujerati has great affective value in relation to personal identity, the use of Urdu is culturally very important to the community although it is little used as a regular means of communication within the family. In all families studied, varying proportions of Gujerati and English were used.

Learning to be literate in home and community

Lengthy interviews with parents and children, informal discussions and observations, visits to homes and schools helped to build up a picture of the experiences of literacy that children had in their everyday environment. Of the 36 children involved in the study, twelve were aged three and a half and just starting at nursery, twelve were aged 7 and twelve aged 11, with equal numbers of boys and girls. The study was built on a matched pair design with half of the children belonging to families who made use of a community centre and half who did not.

At the time of the research (which started in 1996), there were few opportunities for children to use their first language in mainstream school. The Gujerati classes, which had run in two of the seven primary schools involved in the research, had long ceased. When the ILEA was abolished in 1990 and individual London boroughs took over responsibility for education, most of the teachers in the Mother Tongue team were redeployed as teachers of English as an additional language, and many of their community language classes closed. A similar fate befell regular storytelling in these languages. The eurocentric and overloaded National Curriculum of 1988 made no mention of community languages and most teachers felt there was no time in the school day to move beyond its very prescriptive programme.

Of the 36 children in the study, only one had the opportunity to speak in Gujerati to an adult in school, and that was because her aunt was a dinner lady. Most of the schools had a small collection of books in community languages, mainly dual-language story books, and some of these were sent home for parents to read with their children.

Children's literacy experiences in the home

The extent of multiliteracy and the resources encountered by children in the home varied from family to family. The literacy background of parents, the different ways in which the languages of the community were used and the availability of literacy resources, all had an influence on the children's experience of multiliteracy in the home.

About half the parents in the study, like Rehana's, had been educated in India in three languages or more and took multiliteracy completely for granted. This was reflected in the literacy materials in the home, which were primarily in four languages: English, Urdu, Gujerati and Arabic. All families had copies of the Qur'an and some had other religious texts in Arabic. Most families had religious books in Urdu for adults and all had religious books for children in that language, most of which were obtained through the local madressa. Most families had books in Gujerati. Many had magazines and newspapers in Gujerati and some in Urdu. All the children were familiar with the different scripts used for Arabic and Urdu (written from right to left and very similar), Gujerati and English (both left to right).

While common religious books could be obtained from the madressa, a problem for many families was the difficulty of obtaining reading material, especially for children. Friends and relatives travelling to Gujerat were often asked to bring back books. A couple of families bought books in Gujerati by mail order from a company in Leicester, a city in central England with the largest Gujerati speaking population in the country. The literacy materials in these multilingual homes were similar in many respects to those described in studies by Saxena (1994) in a multingual community in Southall, Bhatt (1994) in Leicester, Gregory *et al* (1993) in Tower Hamlets and Kenner (2000b) in London: resources in different languages were used in different areas of children's lives.

Gujerati was the main language used for storytelling, which was a common experience for children, especially the younger ones, in most homes: stories were traditional ones, but a lot of storytelling was spontaneous and related to life in Gujerat, family back home, what happened during the day and significant family events. The shortage of children's books in Gujerati meant that reading to children in that language was less common. Several parents indicated that they appreciated it when the school sent home dual language books in Gujerati.

While some parents reported storytelling in Urdu, that language was primarily used for reading and discussing stories related to the children's religious and moral education, from books obtained from the madressa. When children were old enough to attend religious instruction, at around 6 or 7, this practice became a priority and, in some families like Rehana's, a daily event. While mothers played the lead role in storytelling and reading, in most families, as Gregory found (1998), fathers, grandparents and siblings were also involved. The extent to which different family members were involved in different activities reflected their literacy expertise and family priorities for the children's language development.

Writing letters to relatives in Gujerat was a common activity in many families. Children had homework from school in English and from the Madressa in Urdu. There were a number of examples of 11 year olds helping their parents with business correspondence in English. Other examples included a family who taught their children maths in Gujerati and another whose close relative was an Urdu poet.

The research project showed most families supporting their children to develop literacy in English in the manner recommended by the school. The parents of younger children read story books to them, especially the ones sent home from school. The parents of children aged 7 also provided a great deal of support in both hearing children read regularly and reading to them. There was a tendency for parents to focus these activities on the children who were performing less well in school; good readers aged 7 were encouraged to read by themselves. Children aged 11 at the time of the research project reported reading with their parents regularly when they were younger.

Children's literacy experiences in the community

The family literacy experiences of children showed three languages being used in different ways in children's everyday lives. Gujerati was the most influential language when the children were very young and Urdu became more significant in their lives as religious education became more important. English literacy was encouraged and supported in most families from nursery through to age eleven.

The Cummins model of bilingual development suggests that becoming literate in Gujerati, the first language of the children and the one most used, alongside English, in their homes, would enable children to derive the intellectual benefits of additive bilingualism and perform at a higher level than monolinguals in English. When embarking on this research project, I had wondered whether, in the absence of any form of bilingual education in school, parental and community support for the language of the home would be sufficient to have some impact on children's academic achievement in English. The model did not fit and the reality proved to be much more complex.

There were no Gujerati classes for the children to go to in the neighbourhood since the classes in the mainstream schools, mentioned above, had ceased. While there were a few classes for adults, the community prioritised the learning of Urdu for the children's religious education. Two children were taught to read and write Gujerati at home by their parents, and were the only ones who could properly do so. Some others were taught a little basic literacy at home from primers imported from India. It was very clear from statements made about the affective value of the language, that families wanted their children to learn it and be literate in it, however they were also realistic about the burden of study on their children. Two families in the study mentioned the classes that had once taken place in the mainstream school and several indicated that they would have liked Gujerati to be taught as part of the main-stream curriculum.

All the children in the sample aged 7 and 11 attended madressa on five nights a week for their religious education which took place in Urdu. The following quotation, from a text used at the madressa, spells out the essential religious knowledge and understanding expected of Muslims.

> Muslims must recite the Qur'an in Arabic and learn its meaning in their own lan-guage. (Basic Principles of Islam:15)

From a religious point of view it would be perfectly acceptable for the chil-dren to be instructed in Gujerati or English, but the status of Urdu and tradi-tions in the community ensured that learning Urdu alongside learning to recite the Qur'an in Arabic remained a priority.

Figure 1 on page 32 is an example of a text used to support children's study of the Qur'an. The lines of text in the larger print are written in Arabic. The Urdu translation in smaller print is followed by the English version. Pupils learn the Arabic by heart.

For the children who featured in this study, understanding text was a com-plex, negotiated affair. All the children spoke English, all spoke Gujerati in family and community with varying levels of fluency, all could recite sections of the Qur'an, in Arabic by heart. The texts that support religious and moral education are written in Urdu. Books used are graded for difficulty and one of the first tasks of the children is to learn to read in Urdu from primers.

In the Urdu classes which I was invited to observe, most of the 7 year olds in my study were learning to decode basic Urdu texts: sound-to-symbol corres-pondence is more regular in Urdu than in English and children were learning sounds, 'words that begin with ...', assembling words, decoding, filling in gaps

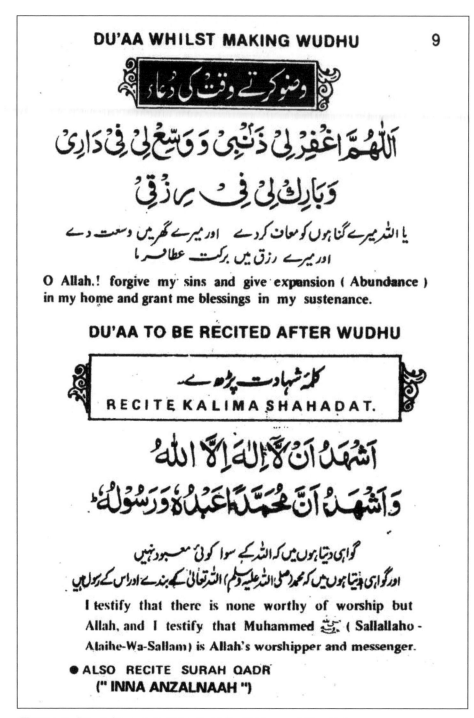

Figure 1: Page from a text in Arabic, Urdu and English
(Basic Essentials for Muslims)

and answering simple questions in writing. The primers used were carefully graded and illustrations were only used in the earliest books. The language of instruction depended very much on the preferred language of the teacher, but was also influenced by the language with which the children were most familiar. Explanations were in Urdu, in Gujerati or in English and the children's responses were also in all of these languages, although not necessarily in a reciprocal manner. In a group of younger children observed, the teacher was a newcomer from Gujerat and the children were using a lot of Gujerati, not only to the teacher, but among themselves, as Rehana reported. A group of older children, working with a young, British-born and fully multilingual teacher, were inclined to use much more English. In conversations with the teacher and, to a much greater extent among themselves, the children were codeswitching.

The ultimate aim was for the children to read the religious texts with understanding and this was achieved through a complex negotiation of three languages. At ages 7, 8 and 9, children were introduced to new Urdu vocabulary through learning words in the context of phrases and sentences and looking them up in dictionaries. Teachers, within the limits of their own linguistic skills, would translate and explain in Gujerati or English. Some children pencilled notes in English in the margins of their text books.

The older children aged 11 and above were expected to learn to read the Urdu texts with understanding. Children observed read in a round and were questioned about the meaning of the text in Urdu. Responses were expected in Urdu, although they were also offered in Gujerati or English. As with many traditional school comprehension exercises, it would have been possible to answer some of the questions by repeating a sentence from the text: a correct answer would not necessarily have indicated understanding. A young teacher, London born and trained in an Islamic boarding school in Bradford, whom I observed teaching a group of the older girls, explained that, when this occurred, she would accept an answer to the question in English. She explained that the children's spoken Urdu was not good enough to discuss the text in any depth and that she could best ensure understanding by asking for paraphrases, explanations or discussion of aspects of character and motivation from the text in English. She would also sometimes ask a very general and open-ended question in English which required a thorough understanding of an entire section of the Urdu text.

Observation of children at age 7 revealed a very wide spread of skills. Some children had learned to decode Urdu text fairly rapidly and one girl was observed translating a simple text confidently from Urdu to English. Others were struggling with the phonics and the simple process of decoding the print. Yet others were decoding fluently but frequently stopping to ask for the meaning of words. In many cases the answer was offered in English or in Gujerati.

By age 11 the children were generally reading for meaning and able to engage in the text level work described above. At all these stages, the children were negotiating meaning in at least two languages at any given time. An able student at the end of the course of study could read basic Urdu with understanding, but few acquired writing composition skills as this was not part of the syllabus taught. For most of the children, Urdu was a language reserved for religious and literary domains. The older children reported to me that, although they may be able to read Urdu with understanding in the context of religious instruction, the vocabulary and style of writing learned tended to restrict their knowledge to that domain. Only those children who regularly used the language for communication in the home had access to a wider repertoire in Urdu literacy. It is generally from this latter group that pupils proceed to study Urdu at GCSE and A level (General Certificate of Secondary Education subject-specific exams, generally taken in the fifth and seventh year of secondary school study) where this is on offer in their secondary school.

Language maintenance and shift

The most interesting part of the investigation for me was working with the children aged 7 and 11 to find out what language they used to whom, where and when. I asked many questions: about parents, grandparents, siblings, extended family, friends in different locations, schools, community classes, play centres etc as well as choice of language in a range of media and for different topics of conversation. Like most bi- and multilinguals, the children used their languages very naturally in different contexts, without being aware of what languages they spoke or whether they were mixing and switching.

The language survey required participants, both adults and children, to make a percentage estimate of how much of each language they would use in conversation with a particular individual or in a specific situation. The questions provoked a tremendous amount of excited debate among the children. A little box with movable cardboard slides in different colours was designed to help the children estimate how much of each of their three languages they spoke in any given situation. There were three colours on the box: the base of the box and the two slides that could be pushed in through the frame from either side. The children could choose which coloured slide to use for which language and move the slides across to estimate how much of each language they used. The researcher then noted a figure by using the (unnumbered) scale at the side. For example, a child might record that she spoke 70% Gujerati, 25% English and 5% Urdu to her father.

As the children manipulated the slides, they thought deeply about their answers and some spontaneously started using percentages. 'I speak about half and half English and Gujerati to my Mum', reported 7 year old Nasima, using the box, 'so that's 50% each. But I talk mostly Gujerati and some Urdu with my Nan, that's about 10% Urdu and 10% English and the rest is Gujerati.' So pleased were some of the 11 year olds with this investigation that they asked to borrow the slide box to carry out their own language use study with their many bilingual classmates.

All the children in the sample were functionally bilingual. When talking in school, in certain community situations and to adults within the family they generally had to respect appropriate norms of language choice: 'it is more polite to speak in Gujerati to grandparents', 'Dad will be cross if I speak in English', 'Mum speaks more in English', etc. It was considered that it was in communication with siblings that the children had the greatest freedom of language choice. Therefore language choice with their siblings was used as a measure of the linguistic vitality of Gujerati in the children's language use (Giles *et al*, 1977).

While there is huge individual variation in children's language use, a broad pattern emerged which confirmed the three-generation model of language shift described by Fishman (1989). Gujerati, English and some Urdu were used in the home. All children reported using mainly Gujerati to their grand-

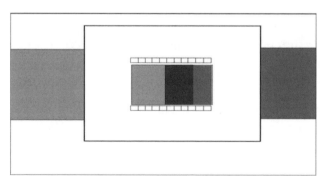

Figure 2: The three-language box (developed by P. Sneddon for this project, 1995)

parents and speaking more Gujerati than English to their parents. While they spoke more English than Gujerati to their siblings, they still spoke a very substantial amount of Gujerati in the home environment. The older the children, the more English they spoke to their siblings and, at all ages, girls used more Gujerati than boys.

The most significant finding of the whole study related to the impact that opportunities to mix socially with other Gujerati speaking children had on the vitality of the language. An investigation of the children's social networks revealed that those who used the community centre and, in particular, the playcentres it organised in school holidays run by Gujerati speaking staff, were far more likely to maintain the use of the language. At age 7, those who used the community centre spoke twice as much Gujerati to their siblings as those who did not. By the age of 11, centre users spoke Gujerati over a third of the time among themselves, whereas non-users of the centre hardly spoke it at all (Sneddon, 2000b).

Observations at the playcentre showed children switching languages according to context as well as tactically: the girls in the role-play beauty parlour putting cucumber slices and tea-bags on their faces spoke to each other in English; when they moved to the corner where they painted Mehendi patterns with henna on their hands, they spoke Gujerati; the boys at cricket practice were shouting to each other in English, but when they played against an English team, they switched to Gujerati.

Language skills and storytelling

Children's oral skills in both English and Gujerati were evaluated in the project through asking them to retell stories. These had been given to them to read with their parents in the home when I visited them with Sakina Hafesji, a Gujerati speaking research assistant. The stories used were *The Very Hungry Caterpillar* (Carle, 1992) with the youngest children, *The Naughty Mouse* (Stone and Desai, 1989) for the children aged 7 and *The Raja's Big Ears* (Desai, 1989) for the older children, all in Gujerati/English versions.

The children varied greatly in their responses to the task, though all but one shy three and a half year old enjoyed the opportunity to record their stories. In a nursery class, Amina was shy with me, but told the story to Sakina in Gujerati. Another nursery teacher had warned me that Omar had not yet spoken in class. However he had met me in his home, he loved the book I had given him and it was from him that Sakina and I got the most wonderfully expressive retelling of *The Hungry Caterpillar* story in both languages.

It was apparent from their recorded narratives that, at age 7, the children's English language skills were still developing. A few children had difficulties with vocabulary that appeared to be unfamiliar in English. In one less fluent speaker's story, '*soldiers*' became '*toldiers*' and '*shoulers*' and '*palace*' became 'place'. The recounts varied from a simple action based narrative focused around illustrations in the book to a lively retelling, with whole passages of expressive and dramatic dialogue. In some instances, where the dialogue revealed developing English skills, the meaning could be slightly unclear '*but he be angry and he was angry still to make me a cap*' but in most cases it did not interfere with pace or meaning: '*I don't sell for the mice, I don't make for mice cloth!*'.

Interestingly, the best storytellers who were most at home with the academic language of the stories were those who also included the colloquial Cockney-influenced east London English (*he done it quick, but he never*) in their tales. Some dramatic narratives were told in Gujerati, with children codeswitching at times into English as they struggled with some of the more literary phrases in standard Gujerati which were unfamiliar to them as dialect speakers. This was particularly noticeable with the repetitive chants in the story which some children found easier to recall in English:

> I'll come in the night with my soldiers as well,
> we'll bite your ears till you squeak, screech and yell

By age 11, the children had achieved good levels of competence in both languages with some distinctive features. Retellings included non-standard colloquial English (*he wouldn't tell no one*) and some features associated with speakers of English as an additional language (*he was burst to tell*); in Gujerati, the children made the story their own, the most lively and creative storytellers being most likely to use dialect and reinterpret the formal language in their own way, making some grammatical errors in the process. As well as codeswitching into English, they sometimes used the same word in both languages, as Rehana did, or created a word such as *baal kapnawalo* (literally *haircutter*) instead of the unfamiliar word for barber, *hajam* (Sneddon and Patel, 2003).

The children's experience of listening to stories told, read and discussed at school, at home and in the Urdu class, was very apparent in the way that many of them structured their tales. Of particular significance was the relationship between the length, structure and depth of stories in both languages: good storytellers in English were also good storytellers in Gujerati. This suggests a transfer of skills operating through the rich and complex pattern of experience of oral and written stories in the children's lives.

Discussion

As a teacher exploring the experiences of children in their homes and communities, I learned a very great deal about the complex negotiations of language that went on in children's homes, in the wider community and in school.

In line with Cummins' concept of the Common Underlying Proficiency, and research findings on the benefits of bilingual education, I was looking for quantitative evidence that the support for Gujerati that children received in the home and the community would have a positive effect on their achievement in English. I did not find this. There was no statistically significant relationship between support for Gujerati and achievement in English. There were no Gujerati classes. The support children received from their families remained primarily oral and, while quite substantial in some cases, was still considerably less than the support given for literacy in English. Urdu, although not regularly used for communication in the home, was the language which all children learned to read as soon as they attended madressa. However, no measures of Urdu achievement were available to me to relate to achievement in English. As mentioned in the introduction, the reality of children's experience was complex. Findings from bilingual programmes in which children became literate in the language of the home did not really apply here.

What I did find, however, in relation to achievement in English was even more complex, and interesting. At age three and a half, there was no clear overall relationship between support for literacy in the home and scores on a Knowledge About Print test. At age 7, gender effects were strong: the evidence of the story recordings showed that the children were generally competent in communicative English, but were still developing as learners of 'book English' (Cummins, 1984). In spite of this, five out of the six girls achieved level two for reading on the Key Stage One tests (the expected level for monolingual English pupils in a test taken at age 7).

By age 11, the evidence of the recordings showed children comfortable with the academic language of books and performing on the London Reading Test, a test of reading comprehension (The London Reading Test, 1992), at a level higher than monolingual pupils of similar social backgrounds. Where the mean for monolingual children in the borough at the time was 100.3, the Gujerati boys scored 106 and the girls 104.5. While this finding does not reach statistical significance, it still demonstrates that the children's considerable achievements in language and literacy knowledge in Gujerati and Urdu had not compromised their achievement in English at the time when they left primary school. Of particular interest is the very unusual finding that the boys' achievement in reading comprehension was ahead of the girls'. As almost all children in the community attend the classes, this may reflect the particularly high status placed in their community on religious knowledge for boys acquired through a close study of texts and complex negotiations of meaning.

Exploration of the children's literacy experiences in the home revealed families who had good relationships with their children's schools. A number reported attending literacy evenings and being given advice on how to support their children at home. They read books sent home from school to the younger children and heard the older children read. Parents tended to focus their energies on children who fell behind with reading. There was a statistically significant relationship in my data between support with reading at home in English and achievement in reading comprehension at age 11 (Sneddon, 2000b).

Literacy practices recommended by the school were increasingly penetrating homes in the area. Teachers in the schools that the children attended were generally positive about the children's bilingualism. However, as Gregory and Williams (2000) and Bourne (2001) have pointed out, there is often little knowledge in school about the language learning and literacy practices of the home, or of what children learn in community classes. The good relations between schools and families operated almost entirely in one direction.

Conclusion

The settings in which children learn outside vary greatly from one community to another and are hard to categorise. Neither 'supplementary school', nor 'complementary school', nor 'mother tongue' nor 'religious school' quite describes the community setting in which the Gujerati Muslim children are learning. While the purpose of their studies is clearly religious, the focus on learning Urdu gives the classes a strong linguistic dimension. Learning at these classes is a great source of pride for the children and their skills form an important part of their personal identities. The pedagogy makes full use of the children's varied linguistic repertoires and operates very differently from the pedagogy of mainstream school. It is not the purpose of these daily classes to support the learning that happens in mainstream school, as is the case in many other forms of complementary education, and the children perceive them as quite separate.

These two areas of learning and the different pedagogies that children experienced every day were very separate in their lives. While most schools are now aware of the languages that children speak, little use is made of their linguistic and literacy knowledge and the complex metalinguistic skills they have learned by exploring meaning across a range of languages in community settings. The parents of the children were not generally highly educated but, taking their grandparents and siblings into account, each family had someone who could read with the children in English and help a little with homework in English, someone who told stories in Gujerati, someone who helped them to learn the Qur'an and read and talked to them about the Urdu texts they brought home from madressa.

It is the children's homes that provide a synthesis: it is there that parents, keen for their children to be successful in school, anxious that they should not lose the ability to speak to their grandparents and wishing them to grow up as good Muslims in the Gujerati tradition, bring the learning together according to family priorities and in whatever language they prefer for the task in hand. Rehana's parents provided a good example of a family successfully providing support for their daughter in ways that mattered to her future as a British Gujerati Muslim.

In the course of the research project, my discussions with children revealed the considerable interest they had in talking about their language and literacy experiences. A closer collaboration between mainstream schools, complementary schools and families would support the children in building on their language skills, their metalinguistic knowledge and their ability to respond to different learning situations and styles. It would thus encourage their development as additive bilinguals.

3

The Story of Bilingual Children Learning to Read

Leena Helavaara Robertson

Introduction

Tell me a story, Pew.
What kind of a story, child?
A story with a happy ending.
There is no such thing in all the world.
As a happy ending?
As an ending.
(Winterson, 2004:49)

This chapter tells the story of five bilingual children who are in the process of learning to read for the first time. The children – two girls, Neela and Saira, and three boys, Amil, Bashir and Ikram (not their real names) – are all of British-Pakistani background. They were born in Watford, England, and their families are from the Mirpur area of Azad Kashmir in Pakistan. At the age of 5 years they are all in the same Reception class of Watford Garden Infant School, having spent a year in the school's nursery. From the Reception year onwards they have a one-hour literacy lesson every morning in which they learn to read in English. Their English teachers talk about the children learning English as an additional language (EAL) because at home they speak Pahari, a language of Azad Kashmir. Bashir also hears and uses some Panjabi at home, and all five already know that Urdu – the national language of Pakistan and different from Pahari – is an important language in their families and community.

Around the time of their 6th birthday, when they are moving on to their Year One class, they have also begun to attend Qu'ranic classes either at the local mosque or at home. The Qu'ran, the holy book of Islam, is written in classical Arabic, and none of the children speak or understand classical Arabic in the conventional sense, but its script resembles that of Urdu. When one of the children, Bashir, spots a dual-language book (English-Urdu) in his English classroom, he says, I do that in the mosque. In the daily Qu'ranic classes the children use little books – as they call them – and first learn to memorise short combinations of letters and phrases. They practise this with careful attention, and little by little they learn to memorise complicated phrases and short paragraphs. It is expected that by the time they are around 7 or 8 years old they can begin to read the Qu'ran.

During this time a local British-Pakistani Ethnic Minority Achievement Grant (EMAG) teacher, Mrs Gani (well known in the school and its surrounding community), establishes an Urdu community school within the Watford Garden Infant School. Along with the rest of the children of British-Pakistani background in this school, Neela, Saira, Amil, Bashir and Ikram attend weekly Urdu lessons that take place during lunchtimes.

And so it is that between the ages of 5 and 7 years, these children have started to read in three different languages. Observing the children move between their literacy classes and focusing on the group organisation begins to reveal some stark differences. In each class the view of the child as a learner is different, and this has a significant effect on what is being taught, deemed appropriate and considered interesting. The children, on the other hand, accept these differences in their stride, codeswitch with ease and considerable skill, and develop distinct chameleon qualities (Miller, 1983).

This chapter tells their story. Or rather, the beginning of their story.

Three vignettes

Some shuffling and fidgeting are going on as one of the Year Two classes settles down and everyone attempts to find their own space on the carpet. Some sit down quickly and copy their teacher's actions and now sit with one finger on their lips to demonstrate that they know how to be quiet and are ready for the lesson. Little by little, everyone begins to pay attention to Mrs Hamilton, the class teacher, who starts the lesson, 'Ooo, you're sitting so beautifully. Let's read this book together. Read with me. From here. Starlight, the stallion, stamps and stumps, in his stuffy stable. Smee, the small smuggler, smiles a small smug smile.' Saira and Bashir repeat some of the words. A while later in another Year

Two classroom, the same text is used, and Amil sits silently and concentrates on looking at the picture of a horse. A daily English literacy lesson has begun.

After lunch, but well before the afternoon lessons begin, all the children of British-Pakistani background in this school gather together for their weekly Urdu lesson. Neela, Saira, Amil, Bashir and Ikram sit on the carpet together with others. Outside, the rest of the school's pupils carry on playing and running about, but inside the teacher, Mrs Gani, asks everyone to remember what kinds of tasks had been completed last week. 'We did the alphabet. Do you remember? Neela, can you remember? Can you do the alphabet for me, we will all help you?' With everyone's help Neela begins to recite the Urdu alphabet, 'Alif, bay, pay, tay, say, jeem... Who's going to come and write this for me? How do you say this in Urdu?'

In the early evening, some time after the school has finished, some children, Ikram and Neela amongst them, come out of their homes again and head towards the local Mosque. Girls wear a hijab, a headscarf, and boys long trousers, never shorts. They arrive with their parents or other family members, and there is much talk and laughter outside the building. Grown-ups exchange news whilst children disappear inside. Boys and girls enter through separate doors and leave their shoes in the entrance hall. Neela kicks off her sandals and goes to a room downstairs, whereas Ikram places his trainers carefully side by side and climbs up the stairs to a different room. In their separate groups and rooms they begin to practise memorising short words and phrases in classical Arabic.

It is not easy to hear Neela's voice but her lips are moving. She reads by looking at and pointing to the text, moves her eyes away from the text, tries to repeat the same phrase, falters, starts again. She repeats it again whilst scrutinising her teacher's face. The teacher suggests improvements and Neela changes her body posture – now she sits taller – and repeats after him. As Neela does not speak or understand classical Arabic, she relies on her teacher's guidance to get it right. This, she knows, is very important and worth striving for. Some older girls have their own Qu'rans on their laps and they read aloud confidently. Upstairs in the boys' room, Ikram has already started reading. He sits up straight and reads on steadily. Soon, from both boys' and girls' rooms, a steady hum of reading can be heard. A daily Qu'ranic reading lesson has begun.

Revisiting the process of learning to read

Learning to read is one of the very central aims of education. Learning to read can also be viewed as a rite of passage, and as such it has been explored time and time again in autobiographical works, memoirs and in literature. Here is

Francie's story, the young female protagonist of The Tree Grows in Brooklyn, who discovers the magic of reading:

> She looked further and when she saw [the word] horse, she heard him pawing the ground and saw the sun glint on his glossy coat. The word running hit her suddenly and she breathed hard as though running herself. The barrier between the individual sound and meaning of the word was removed and the printed word meant a thing at a one quick glance. She read a few pages rapidly and almost became ill with excitement. She wanted to shout it out. She could read! She could read! From that time on, the world was hers for reading. She would never be lonely again, never miss the lack of intimate friends. (Smith, [1943] 2001:166)

Not only is the process of learning to read for the first time frequently written about, it is also much researched, theorised and debated. In fact the acquisition of literacy has gained an all-time high status in terms of political and educational importance. It is viewed as having life-changing qualities – literature confirms and reinforces this – and as Freebody put it, literacy has truly become a modern media superstar:

> Its regular appearances in the media pronouncements on television, in the print media around the world and in literally hundreds of websites attest to its transcendent and heroic status. ... Twenty years ago, Graff (1979) exploded many of these literacy myths [such as improving economy, eradicating ignorance, poverty, crime, consolidating democratic processes] but their durability in the public imagination and the perennial lure they hold for politicians and educational administrators mean that they not only run deep in a generally literate society, but also serve to hold in place certain powerful regulatory, political and ideological systems of surveillance and management. (Freebody, 2001:105)

As the first chapter of this book showed, in Britain literacy – more than any other area or subject – has been right at the very heart of the government's efforts to raise standards in schools in recent years (DfEE, 1998), and its success has been measured by national tests (formerly SATs) and by schools' OFSTED inspections – two of the current systems of surveillance. Much of this emphasis has marginalised bilingual children and their multilingual experiences, knowledge and understanding.

Many of the influential theories and accounts of early literacy have also had a marginalising impact on bilingual children. In general, early literacy theory is based on children learning to read in their first – and only – language (for instance see Goodman, 1969; Clay, 1975; Smith 1985; Bryant and Bradley 1985; Wells, 1986; Adams, 1990; Goswami, 1995). These accounts have not addressed bilingual experiences. And works of literature, such as Francie's story above, play a powerful part in contributing to general consciousness of how this stage of childhood is perceived. The accepted wisdom and the general view in literature, in theoretical models and in the subsequent development of early literacy curricula, and thereby in teachers' professional texts, is that when children learn to read, they do so in one language.

When other languages are considered, the process of learning to read is commonly seen to take place in a new school language, which is not the learner's home or first language. In fact, learning to read in a second language has emerged as a field in its own right. Within this field the emphasis is often on reading materials. Different writers (from Freire in Brazil, to Ashton-Warner in New Zealand, to Edwards and Wallace in Britain (see a useful summary in Edwards, 1997) have argued that, in order to learn to read in a second language, the content of reading materials must be linked with the cultural practices and emotions of readers. Others have examined the transfer of knowledge from one language and literacy to another (Verhoeven, 1987; 1994; Rosowski 2001). Many of these have concentrated on older children and on successive literacies, that is on pupils who have learnt to read in their home language first, and who can subsequently draw upon their previous knowledge and understanding when learning to read in their second or additional language.

The issues raised above are important considerations and yet they do not address the experiences encountered by many young bilingual children. It is rare to find studies that describe a set of *simultaneous* literacy experiences. Hong-Kingston's semi-autobiographical *The Woman Warrior* (1975), is a rare example of literature that shows a young child learning to read in two languages, Chinese and English, in an American school. This is part of Hong-Kingston's story:

> Reading out loud was easier than speaking because we did not have to make up what to say, but I stopped often, and the teacher would think I'd gone quiet again. I could not understand 'I'. The Chinese 'I' has seven strokes, intricacies. How could the American 'I', assuredly wearing a hat like the Chinese, have only three strokes, the middle so straight? Was it out of politeness that this writer left off the strokes the way a Chinese has to write her own name small and crooked? No, it was not politeness; 'I' is a capital and 'you' is a lower-case. I stared at the middle line and waited so long for its black centre to resolve into tight strokes and dots that I forgot to pronounce it. The other troublesome word was 'here', no strong consonant to hang on to, and so flat, when 'here' is two mountainous ideographies. The teacher, who had already told me every day how to read 'I' and 'here', put me in the low corner under the stairs again, where the noisy boys usually sat. (Hong-Kingston, 1975:150)

Like the protagonist here, the children in the opening vignettes are learning to read simultaneously in more than one language and script. This process of learning to read happens once in all their languages; these children do not learn to read three times over. Cummins' (1984) work in Canadian schools and his model of 'Common Underlying Proficiency' is highly relevant here. Within this model Cummins demonstrates how conceptual knowledge and various cognitive skills are transferred from one language to another. For instance, once a concept has been learnt in one language – such as that print carries meaning, or alphabet, or understanding that each spoken word can be segmented into separate phonemes that can be represented by written symbols – the learner does not need to relearn the same concept in another language.

Research on young children and their parallel classrooms has the potential to reveal more about the overall learning processes and the ways in which learning to read is a socially and culturally constructed process. This area has remained largely unrecognised and untapped by teachers, researchers and policy makers. In this context, Gregory's work is groundbreaking (see for example Gregory *et al*, 1993; Gregory, 1994; Gregory *et al*, 2004). Gregory's research has focused on bilingual children of different linguistic and cultural backgrounds and on their processes of learning to read both at home with different family members and in their community language schools, including Qu'ranic classes (Gregory, 1996). She reveals very clearly how all classrooms are domains in which rich funds of knowledge (Moll *et al*, 1992) are being constructed.

Overall, Gregory has been instrumental in shifting some paradigms of knowledge and understanding. The role of older siblings in supporting and teaching young Bangladeshi children to read at home in London's east end, is a case in point, and challenges the conventional and accepted view of family literacy (Gregory, 1998). Children playing school with their siblings (Gregory and Williams, 2000) and teaching each other to read is another interesting dimension of early literacy that is rarely explored in research.

Kenner (2000b, 2004b), too, has worked in this field and has demonstrated how young bilingual children make meaning of different writing systems, and how skilfully they analyse and establish boundaries between different scripts. She expels the myth of different scripts being difficult or confusing for young children, and reveals the energy and delight in which 6 year old children show off their abilities in operating within two separate writing systems.

Many bilingual children are in the process of infusing practices and blending skills and approaches from their different literacy practices. Some studies (Duranti and Ochs, 1996; Volk and deAcosta, 2003; Gregory *et al*, 2004) have highlighted syncretic literacy – mixing and matching both oral and written texts in novel ways – as a pertinent concept for discussing cross-cultural influences. The children are observed to appropriate and syncretise as they go on learning:

> [C]hildren syncretise the languages, literacies, narrative styles and the role relationships appropriate to each group and then go on to transform the languages and cultures they use to create new forms relevant to the purpose needed. (Gregory *et al*, 2004:5)

The five bilingual children

This chapter is based on a larger, longitudinal ethnographic study that set out to discover what kinds of advantages or additional strengths bilingual children might bring from their community literacy practices into their English literacy lessons. Data consisted of field notes, participant observations in the three sets of literacy classes (English, classical Arabic/Qu'ranic and Urdu), audio and videotapes of lessons, and interviews with teachers and parents.

At the start of the study, the Watford Garden Infant School had 226 pupils on roll, of which 15% were of British-Pakistani background. When the five bilingual children were at the start of their Reception year, their teacher, Pippa Lorenzo, provided short descriptions of each:

Neela – 5:3 years

Neela is known for her inquisitiveness and her wish to please and charm adults. She is also good at writing. In whole class teaching situations, she is often quiet and very rarely puts her hand up. She is quick to grasp the topic and seems to understand. Other times she can find herself in trouble for inappropriate behaviour with other children. This has never been serious and takes place at the level of pinching others, when she does not get her way or when she is cross.

Saira – 5:2 years

Saira is a studious pupil, often quiet, with a good fine motor control, who loves to work and play with Megan and Shannon. She is a very gentle little girl, and one who is also inclined to daydream. Sometimes she lacks confidence. In whole class teaching situations she rarely speaks, or offers suggestions, but she always remains on task. She looks, listens, and observes. Saira's English is good.

Amil – 5:3 years

Amil is on the school's SEN register, and there are concerns over Amil's language development. The schools Educational Psychologist has been involved and the subsequent report said that he had limited numeracy skills, unable to count from 10 to 12. Can only recognise numbers between 1-6. Limited literacy skills, can only recognise four sounds. Unable to match letters to objects. Poor expressive language; difficulties in making self clear. Unable to apply his/her/they in context.

The report also said that his mother tongue is weak. When speaking in Pahari his speech is not clear and his mother says that he uses baby talk at home, just like his sister did, before she went to school. Amil, more than any other bilingual child in this class, would benefit from EMAG support, but currently we are not sure what form this should take. Amil is a real little boy, who likes to run outside, muck about. He finds it hard to sit still and is easily distracted. He's also good at distracting others and then gets into trouble.

Bashir – 5:0 years

Bashir is a quick thinker, who works independently. He likes numbers and concentrates very well. Often he likes to help me and put other names up on the board because he can recognise quite a few of them. He knows this is an achievement and that many other children, English children included, cannot read as well as he can. So, he is a high achieving pupil, whose English is terrific. He uses whole sentences and he says things like 'Look, you chopped his leg off', which shows a really good level of English.

Ikram – 5:2 years

Ikram is on the school's SEN register. There have been concerns over his language development. Both his mother tongue and English are weak. His writing skills are poor, his drawings immature, and he has very weak fine motor control. The schools EMAG staff are also worried. Ikram's older brother attends a special school for a global delay in development; and his younger brother may have similar difficulties. In fact there are some serious concerns over Ikram's development. He has some strange rocking behaviour and his speech is slurred. We've involved the speech therapist and are waiting for an assessment. He's a nice little boy, sometimes a bit serious, or dreamy, and he enjoys the computer very much. He also loves to play with other children.

The following sections of this chapter show what happened when the five bilingual children were beginning to learn to read. Observing the children move between their parallel classes and a close examination of each school's organisation of teaching – of groups in particular – begins to reveal some of their story. In each class, the view of the child as a learner is different, and this has a significant effect on what is being taught, deemed appropriate and considered interesting.

Groups in English classes

As in most schools in England, in this school, all classes are divided into smaller groups. Here they are called Green, Blue, Yellow and Red groups, which according to the teachers are based on ability. The teachers say that these ability groups are necessary in order to comply with the recommendations of the National Literacy Strategy (DfEE, 1998) because guided reading – a group reading activity – is structured around different levels of ability, and this organisation will be checked by the school's OFSTED inspectors. Somewhat paradoxically then, guided reading takes place (on average) only once a week in this school, but continues to be the driving force behind the group arrangements for the next two years.

For most of the day, all the children work in their ability groups, and in the English literacy hour lessons (after the whole class teaching) the bilingual children tend to be grouped together. Of the five children, Bashir is the only one to be placed in the Blue Group (second lowest according to Pippa, the teacher) and the rest work in the Green Group, or the lowest ability group, as it is known in the whole school. It is not very clear how ability is defined; the teachers refer to their use of the National Curriculum level descriptors in English and Mathematics (DfEE, 1999a) and measuring children against this set of criteria. But other aspects also influence teachers' perceptions. This becomes apparent as the months go by. For example, a whole year later, when the children are in their Year One class, the overall pattern of these groupings continues unchallenged (see Table 1, page 50).

Red and Yellow Groups, the high ability literacy and numeracy groups, cream off fourteen monolingual children, which is more than half of the whole class. Bashir is the only bilingual child to achieve access into the second highest group, and then only in literacy. None of the others are placed in or move on to a high ability group during their infant school years. It is also important to note that the lowest achieving group has no monolingual learners, and throughout the years the lowest ability groups in the whole school are dominated by bilingual learners.

Table 1: Groups in Year One

Groups (25 pupils in the class)

Ability Groups	Literacy	Numeracy
Red (high)	None of the bilingual children	None of the bilingual children
	Seven monolingual children	Seven monolingual children
Yellow	Bashir	None of the bilingual children
	Seven monolingual children	Seven monolingual children
Blue	Saira, Neela	Bashir, Neela
	Five monolingual children	Five monolingual children
Green (low)	Talib (a boy of Bangladeshi background) Amil, Ikram	Talib, Amil, Ikram, Saira
	None of the monolingual children	None of the monolingual children.

That these groups are not in fact based on ability, or the NC criteria, becomes evident when Bashir begins to overtake many of the monolingual pupils. The class teachers, Pippa and the Year One teacher Jodie Thompson, are the first to acknowledge this, yet this recognition does not enable Bashir to move into the top group. It seems that the main reason for positioning these children in the low ability groups is their language and ethnic background. Their individual levels of English – Saira's and Bashir's English is considered good – are not taken into consideration. All are grouped together as EAL learners from Reception onwards and nothing seems to shift this deficit model.

The Year One Science groups provide further insight into the teachers' views of bilingual children as learners. These groups are called 'Forces' (high ability), 'Senses' (middle ability) and 'Plants' (low ability). The bilingual children are grouped together in the 'Plants' group, which also includes three monolingual children. These group names differ in that forces as a concept is far more complex than senses which again is more complex than plants. Plants are concrete and easily described or illustrated with pictures. The same cannot be said of forces which requires a different kind of scientific classification and thinking. From the onset the teachers' expectations of the bilingual children's academic achievement seem to be lower than that of the monolingual children.

In Year Two, the five bilingual learners are divided between two teachers. Amil as the lowest achieving child moves to Sally Rose's class. Sally is the school's SENCO, and the deputy head, and her class contains many of the struggling learners, the ones who need a bit more support, as she puts it. The rest, Neela, Saira, Bashir and Ikram, are placed in Margaret Hamilton's class, where again Neela, Saira and Ikram are, according to Margaret, in her bottom group and Bashir in the one above that.

The school's groups raise some serious questions. It is important to ask to what extent the teacher's attitudes and their ways of planning for bilingual learners are based on the overall deficit model of bilingualism rather than on the individual children. It is also important to emphasise that when the children are in their Reception class, the school's OFSTED inspection identifies Pippa as an excellent teacher, and Margaret, too, is satisfactory in every way (Sally and Jodie do not yet work at this school). Thus Pippa's classroom organisation is given a very formal validation, and it becomes the blueprint for Jodie, who follows Pippa as the Year One teacher, and for Margaret who follows Jodie. In the main these teachers are following the government's recommendations and aim to raise standards the best they can.

That the two bilingual boys, Amil and Ikram, are grouped in the lowest ability groups throughout their infant years is not, perhaps, surprising, since both of them were deemed to have SEN for language development in their Reception year. In Year One, both boys are still on the SEN register but, as the months go by, Ikram's situation becomes more complex in that he progresses in a very similar manner to the majority of monolingual children in this class. Even though he retains an idiosyncratic way of speaking (according to Pippa his speech is still slurred) this does not signify a delay in language development as documented in his records; moreover, he does not appear to have difficulties in mother tongue and in English. Nor has he any difficulties similar to his older brother who attends a special school. On the contrary, Ikram's attitude and approach are perceived to have developed into something more learning and school-oriented, Sally Rose and Margaret Hamilton comment on it – implying that it was something different when he was in Reception and Year One, and that both Pippa and Jodie are to be congratulated for their very successful teaching. None of the teachers refer to Ikram's own abilities or to his parents, or to his overall bilingualism. Ikram's success is a credit to the school.

In Year Two, all the teachers begin to comment on Ikram's good progress. He is quietly removed from the SEN register, and the fact that he had been there in the first place is a jarring, uncomfortable thought to everyone. The teachers are evasive about the issue: a mistake was made. But Yasmin Hazni, the school's bilingual EMAG assistant, who had contributed to the initial mother tongue assessment, raises this topic several times. Yasmin now feels that she had doubts about this from the beginning, 'I always thought that Ikram was a bright boy, but given the overall constraints of the situation (ie taking the lead from a more experienced head teacher, and thereby welcoming some financial support for Ikram), I had to go along with it.'

Ikram's experiences are reminiscent of Bernard Coard's 1971 study *How the West Indian Child is made Educationally Sub-Normal in the British School System* (Coard, 1971) in which Coard showed how African-Caribbean children were systematically misdiagnosed as educationally sub-normal and classified as having SEN. More than thirty years on, a similar practice flourishes unchallenged.

Amil's story is more sombre still. His difficulties persist from year to year, and the nature of his SEN remains unidentified. The original educational psychologist's diagnosis must be questioned on the grounds that applying 'his' or 'her' inappropriately is a very common learner error with many bilingual pupils, especially if the speaker's first language (like Pahari) has no gendered personal pronouns. This error cannot be used as evidence for poor expressive English.

A motley collection of assumptions are put forward as informal explanations for Amil's difficulties. According to Sally, Amil's Year Two class teacher, his difficulties may be a result of dyslexic difficulties, possibly because of his visual and auditory short-term memory problems. To Margaret (who works in the classroom next to Sally's) his difficulties are best understood in terms of parental involvement ... 'they don't support us', she says. Yasmin talks about his SEN 'he is a slow learner, he's SEN,' but when asked to explain or describe his SEN, she is not sure. Jodie mentions EAL issues, 'it's so difficult for him because of his English.' All of the explanations locate Amil's difficulties within the child, his background and parents, rather than within any possible institutional or school-based factors, or even a mixture of all of these.

It seems that when bilingual children are successful in English lessons, the success is down to their teachers and the school. On the other hand, when they are not successful, the children and their families and languages are to blame. There is a worrying sense of apathy that surrounds Amil, as none of the teachers' explanations are acted upon with a further diagnosis. More teaching support is, however, provided for Amil to meet his carefully defined targets and the support is carefully documented in his records. These targets include some literacy targets, such as to read and write letter sounds 'c, o, a, d, g' and to read by sight the words 'the' and 'and'. None of these targets appeal to Amil himself who enjoys jokes, funny stories, football and running around. When given an opportunity to read with an adult, he pushes – very gently – his own reading book away, and grabs a more enjoyable and challenging story: *Don't Do That!* (Ross, 1993). Amil tells (rather than reads) the story of Nellie who has a very pretty nose (she wins nose competitions), but who also has a nasty habit of sticking her finger up her nose. 'He take it out, yeah, later', Amil explains and points to Nellie whose finger has indeed got stuck in her nose. 'What does that say?' he asks and repeats different words with enthusiasm. Amil, like the rest of the children in this class, is interested in learning to read and in literacies in general.

In Year Two, the five children complete their national tests in English (formerly SATs) and gain the following levels:

Table 2: Test Results in Year Two

Child	English 1/ Reading	English 2/ Reading	English 3/ Writing
Neela	Level two	Level two	Level two
Saira	Level two	Level two	Level two
Amil	Working towards Level one	Level one	Level one
Bashir	Level three	Level three	Level three
Ikram	Level one	Level two	Level two

Level two is considered the average and the required level for Year Two children. Year One children tend to work at level one, and Reception children work towards level one. According to the head teacher, Laura, the results show that Amil is one of the lowest achieving children in the whole school. Bashir, however, is amongst the highest achieving children; a fact that was not acknowledged when the children were designated into ability groups. Neela and Saira, too, achieve the average of their age group (level two) and are no longer amongst the lowest achieving children in their class or school. And as Laura points out, in terms of valued added achievement, Ikram's attainment can be seen as the highest in his class, from SEN register to almost average of his age group.

Perhaps it should be argued that the ability groups have worked, since the four children achieve so well? Other studies (Ireson and Hallam, 1999; Boaler *et al*, 2000), however, provide an overview of ability groups and show how ability groups have no effect on achievement – children do equally well or better in mixed ability groups – but they do have broader negative consequences. Low ability groups tend to set children on a path of dissatisfaction and failure.

To summarise, the number and the nature of the children's first languages are one of the most influential factors in the English teachers' view of the child as a learner. Whether the children are monolingual and English, or, as Swain (1972) put it, they have bilingualism as the first language, has a profound impact. Bilingualism *per se* is perceived as a disadvantage which has overarching consequences and leads to a different style of teaching and low expectations.

Groups in Qu'ranic classes

In the Qu'ranic classes, bilingualism is not an issue. Here everyone is bilingual and all pupils tend to use one or two languages at home, mainly Pahari or Panjabi with their parents and grandparents, and English in their mainstream schools and often with older siblings and cousin-brothers and cousin-sisters. The teachers use mainly Urdu. Pahari wouldn't sound right here, one of the teachers, Mr Khan, says, and Urdu is our language of education.

In some ways, the children start their Qu'ranic lessons at the same level: the majority of children do not use Urdu at home, though they may hear it through satellite TV channels such as Zee-TV, or they may hear newspapers being read in Urdu. In addition, none of the children know or understand classical Arabic, the language of the Qu'ran. In Islamic tradition, an important part of being a believer is the ability to read and recite the Qu'ran, regardless of languages spoken or understood. Each learner is, therefore, in the same situation and will begin to learn to read texts written in classical Arabic by memorising intricate phoneme-grapheme relationships. They will learn by relying on their rote learning skills. This act of reciting is more than an enjoyable repetition of words and phrases. Scribner describes it as:

> Memorizing the Qu'ran – literally taking its words into you and making them part of yourself – is simultaneously a process of becoming literate and holy. (Scribner, 1984:13)

The majority will never learn to understand the texts themselves, but all will learn to describe what the texts are about. Many children will attend other types of classes, too, which tend to take place during school holidays. Within these additional mixed classes – boys and girls attend together – the children do not learn to recite the Qu'ran, but instead to understand its message and its place in their lives.

Unlike in the English classes, where the gender differences are more implicit, in the Qu'ranic literacy lessons in the mosque, the gender differences are made very explicit. The boys and girls read separately and have slightly different rules for reading. Older boys, for example, are encouraged to chant whilst they read, whereas girls read more quietly. In fact, gender seems to be one of the most influential factors affecting the classes, teaching and the styles of reading. Consistently more boys attend. The number of boys attending the evening Qu'ranic classes tends to be between 28 and 38, whereas about six to fifteen girls attend the same evening classes. The boys' class is taught by Mr Khan and the girls by Mr Aziz. In the daytime holiday classes, in which the understanding of Qu'ran is also taught, the difference is similar: about two to six girls and eighteen to twenty-four boys attend.

Mr Aziz says there is a strong correlation between the overall English school achievement and the Qu'ranic reading. Those who do well at the English school are often born brainy, and they do well in the mosque classes, too. Some will never read very well, but everyone can try, learn at their own pace. It seems that when children are successful in the Qu'ranic lessons, the success is down to a number of factors: teachers, lessons, the children themselves, their families, and ultimately their god, Allah, who has blessed some to become brainy. And when they are not successful, if they have attended classes regularly and tried their best, the children themselves are exonerated. It's not their fault – they have other blessings, Mr Aziz says. But if they have been lazy, then both the children and their parents are to be blamed for the failure.

In order to encourage the girls further, one of the youngest boys, Bilaal, who is 5 years old, is asked to demonstrate his reading to the girls, some of whom are around 13 or 14 years old. Neela is amongst them. Whilst Bilaal is not the best or the highest-achieving male pupil, his ability to read and recite long verses and to read accurately is astounding. It also turns out that he is Mr Khan's son. It is expected that Bilaal's reading will motivate the girls. The opposite, high-achieving girls demonstrating and inspiring boys, does not appear to take place.

Ikram, Amil and Neela attend these Qu'ranic classes fairly regularly and, as in the English school, both Ikram and Neela are making good progress. Amil, on the other hand, is considered somewhat lazy, and Mr Khan, the boys' teacher, says that Amil has not learnt as much as Ikram. Saira reads occasionally at home with her mother. Bashir practises both Qu'ranic and English reading at home and is said to attend a different set of classes in Watford, where he is making good progress.

In the Qu'ranic classes, the view of the child as a learner is undoubtedly affected by gender. Some of the observations suggest that the expectations of the boys are different from those of the girls. The Watford families seem to ensure that their sons attend more regularly than their daughters and for a longer period in their lives. But there are other complicating factors involved that are outside the focus of this study. For example, it may simply be that girls prefer to read more at home since in the Islamic way of life there is a long tradition of the women reading at home whilst the men read at the mosque.

What is striking is that the pupil's age, language background and bilingualism are not significant factors. All learners, bilinguals and monolinguals, are viewed as independent and disciplined readers (with boys perhaps being awarded more respect than girls). Everyone's learning process rests on their own level of self-discipline. It is important to pay attention, to concentrate and to get the reading of each passage absolutely right because it cannot be complemented with an individual's comprehension of it. At the age of 5 years the children talk very readily about doing it properly and not cheating. They are fully aware of the level of self-discipline required (Robertson, 2006).

In these classes, children are expected to demonstrate willpower and honesty from the earliest age onwards. They are not placed in any ability group as this would go against the principles of Qu'ranic reading. It is easy to cheat, to read sloppily, to mumble, to skip phrases, but children are encouraged to take control of their own progress, to show that they can read independently and with integrity. Some aspects of independence and autonomy awarded to individual learners are far greater than in the English class. The learners are expected to take control over their own learning and to manage and be in charge of their own individual lesson.

For the children, the start of these lessons and the individual act of reading is deeply meaningful. It is about growing up and about empowerment. Their parents and elders trust in their being considered capable of succeeding with the highly individual and challenging task of memorising the Qu'ran is, first of all, exhilarating as well as empowering. It is about learning to belong to their community, about accepting and negotiating its values and about understanding its collective and shared experiences that have long historical roots. It is a rite of passage.

Groups in Urdu classes

In Watford, the first Urdu classes were started in 1981 by four qualified teachers in two local schools, and soon nearly 100 children attended (Hussain, 1982). However, rarely have these Watford classes existed consistently, although there are some exceptions. Generally, they have been vulnerable to a number of changes, from the macro level (for example the Swann Report (DES, 1985) and the Education Reform Act, 1988 (HMSO, 1988)) to the local, micro level (for example new head teachers terminating classes). The Urdu schools and lessons can easily cease to exist and are totally dependent on the goodwill of teachers.

In addition, many community language schools suffer from prejudices because their teachers draw on different cultural practices. Their teaching is based on different pedagogical styles and understandings which, in turn, are based on very different historical traditions. This is particularly true of the British-Pakistani community which, after the September 11 2001 attacks in the USA, has experienced an increased level of misunderstanding. In English schools, there is an often-held assumption that community language schools are rigid, formal and old-fashioned in their approach, that they are stuck in bygone teaching methods.

The Urdu classes are different from both English and Qu'ranic classes. The children's bilingualism (Pahari and English) is a starting point for learning Urdu, and much time and effort is spent on translating between the three languages, and on fostering individuals' comprehension, response and interpretation of meaning. Bilingualism is seen as a valuable, sought-after, positive phenomenon. In these classes everyone is bilingual.

Zara Gani, a local peripatetic EMAG teacher, spends one lunchtime each week on these lessons. The English schools head teacher, Laura Grendon, and deputy head, Sally Rose, are both highly supportive of her work; they both value Urdu lessons and consider them important for the school's British-Pakistani pupils. Sally would also like to see some English children attend these classes – she values bilingualism – and even though the classes are open to everyone, only one boy, Luke, attends.

Zara plans and prepares the curriculum, lesson content and resources herself as the weeks progress, and as she gets to know the children. Unlike the English teachers, who sometimes feel straitjacketed by SATs, OFSTED and the literacy hour, Zara has flexibility and freedom. She searches for ideas and activities as she rushes from school to school, and selects and makes resources that fit in with her plans and the pupils' interests. She is in charge and she plans ahead, but sometimes changes her mind on the spot, and abandons all plans. She appreciates the freedom but also notes that it comes with a price. In the context of education, a curriculum and a set of lessons that are officially endorsed by government bodies, are formally validated. Schools that are not are generally perceived as less professional and valuable.

Zara would welcome more formal endorsement, as that might ensure consistency and perhaps enable her to hold these lessons during school hours, and not during marginalised lunchtimes. As it is, she has limited resources, no one to support her, and the lessons rest on her energy. In some ways, Zara is a pioneer, a lonely pathfinder of community language provision, who remains hopeful that soon she will find someone to take over the teaching of these classes. Until such time, she remains firmly dedicated to this generation of British-Pakistani children. The English school system does not provide support for home language development, maintenance or revitalisation, so communities have had to become active, and remain assertively active over many decades. Zara feels strongly about the need for these children to learn Urdu, the national language of their other home. Zara says, 'it's almost like teaching a foreign language, the children do not yet know many Urdu words'.

Because of the constraints on Zara's time, the bilingual children are grouped together; there are no ability groups. On average around 20 children between the ages of 5 to 7 years attend every week, and they work together. The lessons, often lasting around 30 to 40 minutes, follow the structure of the mainstream literacy hour lesson. The whole group sits together facing a big book or the whiteboard and children engage in talking, practising, reading, writing and, above all, translating from English to Pahari to Urdu and back again. This is followed by some writing tasks that are the same for everyone. Just like the literacy hour lessons, every Urdu lesson ends in a plenary, a summary of what has been discussed and learnt.

But the Urdu lessons also have a different feel to them. Zara emphasises that this is a club, not really a class and that she tries to have a lot of fun with the children, and finish before playtime ends, so that they have a chance to run around as well. She feels guilty that the children miss their playtimes. She returns to fun and says 'I want them to see it as a club.' She maintains that she is not very strict and sometimes the noise level goes up. 'They like it, I want them to enjoy it.' The need to belong to a club and have fun are directly linked with the general perceptions that linger around community language schools. The raised noise level tends to be accepted as proof that Zara's teaching style is not formal, strict or old-fashioned.

That Zara feels guilty for enabling children to learn another language, important in terms of their identity and cultural background, is astonishing. In fact, it is surprising how many different aspects of language, script systems or language use are referred to and addressed in all Urdu lessons. Here, for example, everyone's attention is on onomatopoeia and they consider how onomatopoeia is language-specific (here 'T' refers to translation and 'TL' transliteration):

Table 3: Onomatopoeia in the Urdu class

	Children		Teacher	Notes
72			A special word?	
73	All	Crunch, crunch	Crunch, how do you say that in Urdu? ـکچَر [T: CRUNCH]	{TL: Kachar}
74	All	ـکچَر ـکچَر ـکچَر T: CRUNCH, CRUNCH,CRUNCH]		{TL: Kachar, Kachar, Kachar.}

All languages have onomatopoeic words, but in each language these are based on its own particular rules of phonology and morphology. English 'crunch' and Urdu 'kachar' sound similar and have similar plosive phonemes, such as 'k'. They also have similar, but not the same 'r' sound. Zara points out some of these differences, and repeats both the English 'crunch' and the Urdu 'kachar' and notes that when discussing eating in Urdu, it would be difficult to use the English word 'crunch'. The children laugh and continue to call out 'kachar, kachar'. It is probable that Zara's intention is not to explore or negotiate the meanings of these terms at this level. However, given the fact that translation is a complex process, and sometimes words do not translate into other languages in a simple, direct way, almost by default, the act of translation will include careful and critical reflection. Meanings of words are understood as language-specific.

The act of translation, Zara switching from one language to another, and asking the children to repeat or think about words in Urdu, regularly introduces these other additional elements. The levels of analysis throughout the Urdu lessons are higher than Zara, perhaps, intends, but this enables her to maintain high academic expectations of all pupils. The classroom discussions are serious, academic and challenging.

Zara is pleased that everyone has had some opportunities to learn Urdu, and she talks about everyone being a successful learner. She does not view this success in terms of fast individual progress, or raised levels of individual achievement or individual targets being met. To Zara, success is a result of joint and shared participation. The children are successful learners because they have engaged in learning Urdu.

Conclusion

As the years go by, Neela, Saira, Amil, Bashir and Ikram all begin to learn to read. The children's bilingualism – in English and Pahari – is seen as a significant factor in both English and Urdu classes, and it contributes strongly to the teachers' views of children as learners. The English teachers perceive bilingualism as a disadvantage, which leads to low expectations and labelling bilingual children as low ability, EAL children. The Urdu teacher, on the other hand, views bilingualism as an advantage and a starting point for beginning to learn a third language, Urdu. The observations challenge the myth of community language classes being old-fashioned and rigid and the mainstream English classes being inclusive; in fact the observations reveal that the English classes were highly rigid and exclusive.

In the Qu'ranic classes, bilingualism is not a significant factor. Regardless of languages spoken or understood, everyone is expected to learn to read the Qu'ran. The children accept all these differences between their literacy classes – ie the different group systems, roles of readers, implicit and explicit rules and a range of procedures – in their stride. They seem to have a heightened need to make sense of their literacy classes at the time when they are learning to decode texts and meanings. Rather than confusing children, these parallel experiences seem a powerful force in their progress, and they show willingly that they know how you have got to do it in each (Robertson, 2006).

Codeswitching – switching between languages and cultures – is an everyday part of their lives, and this kind of situated knowledge of school learning is acquired very early on. They know exactly how reading is done in each class, and the regular movement between their parallel classes facilitates the children to accrue their true chameleon qualities. It is possible that becoming and remaining multilingual and multiliterate can take place in homes. However, this chapter has also argued that, since English schools do not provide opportunities for the development, maintenance or revitalisation of community languages, becoming multilingual and multiliterate is greatly supported by community language schools. They facilitate the shared and social contexts in which both linguistic and cultural fluency can flourish.

But what happened then to Neela, Saira, Amil, Bashir and Ikram?

At the age of 8 years, they move on to their junior school – a much larger school and building – and start another phase of their schooling, Key Stage Two. They continue to be seen as EAL pupils and receive some EMAG support. Highly unusually, however, this junior school has had Urdu lessons in operation consistently since 1987, and these lessons take place during school hours, not lunchtimes or after-school hours. It is probable that here they will meet up with some old friends from their Qu'ranic classes and that they will continue to explore the myriad and diverse intricacies between different languages.

Zara Gani, however, can no longer juggle her increasing workload and find time for the infant school Urdu lessons. The head teachers, Laura and Sally, continue to search for someone who could take over the teaching. So far they have not been successful, but Laura remains positive and mentions some new, young mothers, who might be interested. And so, another new school year begins. Another group of young children start their Reception class, all of them almost 5 years old. Some of them run across the schools lawn and skip into the school building. Some have to be pulled inside. Ikram's younger brother is amongst these children, and so begins another story.

4

Contributing to Success: Chinese parents and the community school

Yangguang Chen

Introduction

While numerous studies have been devoted to identifying the various causes responsible for educational under-achievement since the 1960s, the issue of the school performance of ethnic minority children in Britain continues to puzzle educationists and to cause anxiety to many ethnic minority parents as well. There are few studies focusing on the successful education of ethnic minority children, particularly of Chinese minority children who continue to be prominent among the high achievers within the British education system (DfEE, 2001). The Chinese experience of British education and the possible reasons for their success have been overlooked in research.

The study on which this chapter is based investigated Chinese students and their success in education in Britain, focusing on parental involvement in their children's education and on the role of community schools. This chapter addresses three main questions:

- What are Chinese parents' attitudes towards education in Britain, and what strategies do parents use in order to combat disadvantage and ensure their children's success in education?

- What role do Chinese community schools play in Chinese children's educational performance?

- What benefits does this form of schooling bring about for Chinese children?

Background to study: parental involvement

The study presented in this chapter draws on a growing body of research published during the last thirty years into how the home plays a major role in children's educational achievement. Two important factors considered here are the involvement of parents, and the role of weekend community schools.

Since the Plowden Report, the importance of parental involvement in education has been recognised. Research into relations between the home and school has focused particularly on perceived problems in the relationship between educational institutions and parents of low social class background, as well as non-English speaking, ethnic minority parents. This chapter explores the positive role of ethnic minority parents in their children's education.

In spite of the stereotypical and prejudicial views about ethnic minority parents and the role they play in their children's education, the 1970s saw a shift away from the view that non-English speaking minority parents were a problem. The claim that ethnic minority parents held certain attitudes or brought up their children in certain ways which made it difficult, or even impossible, for schools to do their job properly, was rejected. It was recognised that parents should not be blamed for their children's under-performance in schools. For example, Rex and Tomlinson (1979), in their study of African-Caribbean and Asian parents in Birmingham, found that educational background did not have a bearing on parents' expectations in that most parents shared a high expectation about education, and viewed schools as places where their children's life chances should be enhanced.

Evidence emerged that students were, on the contrary, disadvantaged by racial discrimination and by poor socio-economic circumstances, and also handicapped by insufficient knowledge of the school system. The parents did take considerable interest in their children's education, and expected their children to do well, and aspired for them to succeed by gaining qualifications and jobs. As noted by Tomlinson (1984:52),

> many migrant parents working in low-paid jobs have felt that their efforts might be justified if their children could acquire a more favourable position in society than they were able to achieve.

Other research in the 1980s which focused more on specific groups of ethnic minority parents, continued to support the conclusions that minority parents expect schools to provide qualifications, a work-oriented education and respect for cultural, religious and linguistic differences – and that schools sometimes find difficulty in meeting these expectations. This research highlighted the fact that parents did indeed have high expectations, and also that teachers lacked knowledge of minorities and their backgrounds, and thus tended to have low expectations of the children's educational capabilities (Ghuman, 1980; Bhachu, 1985; MacCleod, 1985; Smith and Tomlinson, 1989).

The research literature does, however, demonstrate that ethnic and cultural differences do add an extra dimension to issues of parental involvement. Indeed, some minority parents may not be able to help their children with the school curriculum and with their reading or homework as other parents do. However, there are many other areas in which they do provide support. Of major importance are constant encouragement and a supportive attitude to school and these are significant factors in their children's learning (Topping, 1986). Studies have further supported the conclusion that parental involvement for minority parents can take place in many ways and that 'coming from an ethnic minority does not necessarily lead to educational disadvantage or low achievement' (Tomlinson and Hutchison, 1991:4). In their report on Bangladeshi parents and education in Tower Hamlets, Tomlinson and Hutchison (1991:3) conclude that:

> failure to acknowledge the importance of parental involvement would lead in some cases, to teachers blaming parents for undesirable influences, an inability to assist their children educationally, and also to some parents, blaming schools for failing to equip their children with appropriate skills and qualifications.

In Tomlinson's (1984) research in Birmingham, she found that West Indian parents displayed an interest in education equal to that of Asian parents. However, their own educational experiences have tended to leave them with confused expectations of the educational system in their adoptive country and therefore they are reliant on the schools taking the initiative in encouraging involvement (Tomlinson, 1984). What is noticeable, she warned, is that:

> ... more educational researchers, particularly those of Asian origin themselves (Dosanjh, 1969; Bhatti, 1978; Ghuman, 1980) have stressed the positive interest and characteristics of Asian families; while white researchers attempting to explain poor West Indian school performance, have often stressed supposedly negative family characteristics. (Tomlinson, 1984:52)

All in all, research literature over the last thirty years has shown that perspectives and ideologies about the role of ethnic minority parents have changed a great deal. However, with regard to the Chinese community in Britain there is very little in-depth information. There is limited specific research on Chinese parents' involvement in their children's education. The reasons often cited for the absence include the relatively small number of Chinese children in British schools, the reserved nature of the Chinese ethnic group, most parents working unsocial hours in the catering business and difficulties in locating qualified and experienced bilingual and bicultural researchers (Tomlinson, 1984; Taylor, 1987; Li Wei, 1994).

What we can mostly see from very limited data (Broady, 1955; Ny, 1968; Jones, 1979; Watson, 1977; Wang, 1982) presented by either white researchers or those of Chinese origin themselves is about the largely negative documentation of some supposed family characteristics, for example, low expectations, reluctance to accommodate to the majority society, desire to preserve a cultural separateness, and a lack of urgency to learn English.

Only in more recent years do we come across literature which is more positive (for example, Wong, 1992; Li Wei, 1994; Pang, 1999; Parker, 2000; Chau and Yu, 2001; Francis and Archer, 2005). This, more recent literature, documents, among other things, Chinese parents' high educational and occupational aspirations for their children. Other studies (Gregory, 1993; Li Wei, 2000; Ran, 2000; Li and Rao, 2000; Kenner, 2004b) centre on the exploration of Chinese literacy practices in the homes of Chinese families and the parental contribution to this process. However, little is known of Chinese parents' attitudes towards mainstream education and their active involvement in children's academic success. The present study, therefore, aims to reveal parents' thoughts and strategies with regard to these matters.

Community schools

As noted in Chapter One in this volume, schools set up by communities have a long history in Britain, and the growth of such schools has been coupled with a wider acceptance of the principle of parental involvement.

The first Chinese class started in 1928 at a restaurant in London and, after acquiring its own premises in East London in 1934, it developed into the first Chinese school, named Chung Hua Chinese School (Ny, 1968; Jones, 1980). The late 1960s and early 1970s saw the expansion of Chinese supplementary schools, schools in which classes generally took place on Saturdays and Sundays.

A powerful motivation behind such schools has been the desire to retain cultural identity, which in most cases is very strongly linked with the retention of a mother tongue and cultural heritage. Chinese parents in Britain, in particular, face the problem of retaining a linguistic identity which will allow all generations within a family to communicate with each other, while at the same time ensuring that the children can operate in the language of the mainstream society. The desire was fuelled by the EEC directive of the mid-1970s, which began to see children's home language as a positive asset of multicultural education and charged its member countries with a responsibility to ensure that mother tongue and cultural teaching were available to minority children.

The EEC directive certainly stimulated debate in Britain as to how far such teaching should be provided in schools, and how far minority communities should take the initiative. The DES favoured community initiatives, and considered that children's home language should be fostered, but not incorporated in any general way into mainstream teaching. Mother tongue teaching within the mainstream was seen as worth developing only when ethnic languages may become a subject within the curriculum but not a medium in teaching the curriculum. The minority communities therefore were themselves directly responsible for their own linguistic, religious and cultural needs, and voluntary self-help schemes were encouraged by offering Local Education Authority premises to community groups for their classes (DES, 1985). Consequently, many new mother-tongue schools were established by community groups themselves during this period and these have usually been referred to as community schools.

According to the *Resource Unit for Supplementary and Mother-Tongue Schools* (RUSMTS), there are over 2000 supplementary schools across the UK, yet these schools have received a disproportionately small amount of attention from researchers and educationalists alike; their practices have been little documented by researchers (Martin *et al*, 2004). What has mostly appeared in the literature about community schools are simplistic accounts showing that these schools are extremely diverse in both form and purpose (Tomlinson, 1984); some are funded or given premises by LEAs, others are self-sufficient; and teachers are mostly unqualified volunteers (Wong, 1992; Ran, 2000). Little is documented about the role that these schools may play in their children's academic achievement.

Chinese community schools, in particular, have rarely been examined despite the fact that Chinese children are generally high achievers. Due to various historical reasons and the mainstream stereotypes, the Chinese community is known as the silent minority (Chann, 1984, cited in Wong, 1992). It is only in recent times that attempts have been made to shed light on the identities and attitudes to education among high-achieving Chinese communities in the British education system. The findings have shown the value placed on community schools by Chinese children and parents, and the pivotal role that community schools actually play to meet various expectations of Chinese parents in Britain. However, what needs to be further explored is how Chinese schools are perceived by students, and how complementary schooling has contributed to their academic achievement. The current study provides such an exploration.

Settings and participants

The setting for this study is London, where ethnic minorities comprise 29 percent of all residents, of whom 56,579 are Chinese, making up 28 percent of the total Chinese population in Britain. The study focuses on children's homes and Chinese community schools. Participants include three younger children of two newly arrived families and five older bilingual children coming respectively from the London Mandarin School and the Republic Chinese School. The sample also consists of their parents.

Three emergent bilingual girls of two newly arrived families

The two families, who have arrived recently in the UK, come from very different backgrounds. They represent two different groups of Chinese new immigrants. The Mandarin-speaking family is from mainland China. The parents are university graduates although their spoken English is not fluent. They are studying at the City University of London. They represent thousands of Chinese parents in mainland China today who want to prolong their stay abroad at all costs just for the sake of their children's education. Shan, their daughter, who is 10 years old, joined them a few months ago. In line with her age, Shan was placed in Year Six the first day she entered a primary school situated in the Islington area. No language support teacher was available, so it was suggested that Shan join the Year Three class for her English literacy, the Year Five class for her Maths lesson, and stay with her own class for the rest of the curriculum.

The Cantonese-speaking family is from Hong Kong. The parents, like the majority of early immigrants from Hong Kong, came to work in the kitchen of a restaurant in Chinatown or a Chinese take-away. They have had little education and are totally illiterate in English. Their two daughters, Wington and Kapo came to join them a short time ago, and they are now studying at a parish school in the Soho area. Kapo, aged 11, is in the Year Six class while Wington aged 8 is in Year Four. There is a language support teacher who works part-time in the school. According to her teacher, Wington stayed with children in Year One for literacy lessons every morning, and occasionally joined a small group of the Year Three children with learning difficulties. The elder sister was said to be fine in her Year Six class, and once a week went to the language support teacher for half an hour's tuition.

Life in the mainstream class, as observed, is organised around specific targets set up in the National Curriculum. Everyone in the class is given the same instruction and does the same class work which, most of the time, would be based around teamwork. Shan, Kapo and Wington are no exception but are withdrawn from some class lessons. They spend time in their own class and are also sent to younger classes for some subjects. Classroom observations reveal that they have experienced considerable disadvantages leading to feelings of isolation, misunderstandings and frustration. Particularly, data show that the children want desperately to get extra help, but this appears not to be fully understood by their teachers. Language support does take place occasionally but it is always mingled with learning support. Even so, the support is still very limited as there are hardly any full-time support teachers in schools. Due to financial constraints, even the numbers of part-time support teachers have been reduced. This has caused problems for these emergent bilingual children.

Although the schools have attempted to include these three children in order to ensure equality of opportunity, they are excluded from their chronological age group for literacy and numeracy work. This situation worries both sets of parents and the mismatch of their expectations with what schools actually offer has led to several self-help strategies.

Five older bilingual girls from two community schools

Susan Wu, Joyce Chen, Nicola Xian, Ying Ma and Joe Woods are five GCSE students, aged 13-15. They came to the UK with their parents when they were approximately 7-9 years old. They speak Chinese at home, and each has come to London Mandarin School or Republic Chinese School to continue their literacy development in Chinese and participate in many extra-curricular activities. Being brought up in a bilingual environment, they are thus fluent in both Chinese and English. They are doing very well, not only in their Chinese lessons but also in their English schools. They have recently completed GCSE Chinese studies with A* and have gone on to achieve exceptional GCSE grades in their English school, having a string of As and A*s to their names.

London Mandarin School opens every Sunday while Republic Chinese School runs on Saturday. The curricula in these two schools all centre on language, literacy, cultural transmission and supplementary subject teaching but they differ in their medium of instruction. While London Mandarin School teaches in Mandarin, Republic Chinese School teaches in Cantonese. According to Mr Ho, the headteacher in Republic Chinese School, a Mandarin class has been set up recently for some Cantonese-speaking kids who are expected to learn Chinese taught in Mandarin because their parents think that it would be more useful for their future careers if they could speak Mandarin.

For clarity, when referring to medium of instruction – Mandarin or Cantonese – we are referring to dialects spoken in different areas. There are several misconceptions about the Chinese language and it is important to point out that Cantonese is just one of the eight major dialects of the Chinese language across the country and overseas. Although different dialects vary immensely in pronunciation, they share the same written forms. Mandarin is based on the pronunciation of the Northern dialects (which have many sub-dialects) and are spoken by 80 percent of the Chinese population. Therefore it grew to become the national language (*Guoyu*) in the Republican period (1912-1949), a term still used in Taiwan and some Chinese communities outside the mainland. In the People's Republic the name for it is 'common language' (*Putonghua*), and it is taught in schools and spoken by television and radio presenters in mainland China. Cantonese, as it is spoken by generations of the first Chinese immigrants from Canton and Hong Kong, has developed into a dominant dialect overseas.

Relatively speaking, London Mandarin School is a young school set up only six years ago, while Republic Chinese School was founded 20 years ago. Both schools have six classes from Year 1 to GCSE, but London Mandarin School has recently opened an A level class. Being independent of any LEA in London, and due to lack of funding, London Mandarin School's site changes frequently. It was at first housed in one of the churches in Soho, then moved to the London Business School in Fulham, and is now at Babage Primary School in the area of Old Street. Nevertheless, the school still attracts many children from all over London and the outskirts.

The case is different with Republic Chinese School, which is permanently housed in Westminster College near Chinatown and is funded by the Chinese Community Centre in the area. Usually children like to drop in at the Centre before and after class, watching videos and playing table tennis or chess, and they will never miss any annual festival celebration parties held by the Centre.

In London Mandarin School, extra-curricular activities can only be arranged through some organisations and mostly through personal contacts. Teachers and parents work closely to find opportunities for children.

Most teachers in the two schools are parents themselves. In Republic Chinese School, teachers were students from Hong Kong and now are UK citizens working in various professions, while in London Mandarin School, teachers are from among those mainland Chinese who first came to the UK as students and scholars with the open-door policy of the late 1970s. Children and spouses began arriving as dependents from the 1980s. Many who came as students in the 1980s then found themselves parents in the 1990s. They mostly graduated from universities, especially the men, many of whom completed doctoral studies. They are very keen on their children's education and offer to become volunteer teachers.

Despite the fact that teachers in both London Mandarin School and Republic Chinese School do not have teaching certificates, their educational background, age and enthusiasm have given them confidence in the education of Chinese students. The advantage with these teachers is that they are all bilingual and, after having experienced life in Britain, are more able to consider some of the cultural conflicts faced by Chinese children in Britain. Such knowledge in fact has helped teachers to fulfil their responsibilities and eliminate some of the culture shock experienced between parents and children.

In order to meet the needs of pupils and achieve efficiency in teaching the Chinese language to children in Britain, English is used in addition to Chinese in the classroom. Bilingual teaching is encouraged in the classroom for comprehension purposes, and this attracts many Chinese children and some English-Chinese mixed families in particular.

Findings
The parents' attitudes towards education and their knowledge of British schools and teachers

As mentioned earlier, the two families who arrived recently in the UK come from very different backgrounds. They differ considerably in terms of educational background, but they all share Confucius heritage culture and Confucius' perception of man, knowledge and society, and believe that education is of paramount importance in all societies and that success in education will lead to occupational and status mobility.

Therefore, both sets of parents came to Britain expecting to improve the education and life chances of their children. They both held high aspirations for their children's success in education. They were critical about their own educational experience and found many problems with their home education system. Although they differed in their knowledge of the English education system, they all believed that English education would provide more opportunities and would lead to social and economic advancement. They also assumed that English teachers would have high expectations for their pupils. In informal interviews, the parents made the following comments, which reflect their different access to knowledge about education.

Excerpt One – Parents from Hong Kong

1   Author: What has brought about your decision to move to this country since Hong Kong is quite a good place?

2   Mum: Well, Hong Kong is overcrowded; there are too many people and limited job opportunities.

3   Author: But the education in Hong Kong is also quite advanced.

4   Mum: But schools put too much pressure on children, too much homework, too much for kids.

5   Author: Were they doing well over there?

6   Mum: They were generally okay, but not out of the common run. So we thought it would be quite risky for them to move up.

7   Author: Do you expect them to go to university here in Britain?

8   Mum: Yes, of course. We did not study much when we were young, and now we cannot find a good job.

9   Author: What do you mean by a good job?

10   Mum: Well, some jobs in the office, work fewer hours but get paid more. In Hong Kong those office jobs either in the company or in the civil service are normally filled by university graduates (*sighs*). Life is hard on us because we did not have a good education, but we want our children to be better off than us.

11   Author: How much do you know about Britain?

12   Mum: Well, at least Britain has less population, more opportunities, and money is better valued.

13   Author: What about the schools here?

14   Mum: I think schools here should be better than Hong Kong's as Hong Kong has been following Britain, am I right? And people in Hong Kong all say: British education is better valued and less competitive.

15   Author: Does your husband have the same idea?

16   Mum: Yes, my husband said that since so many rich people were mad about sending their children to British 'A' level colleges or universities at very high expense, why don't we make use of this opportunity while being employed here?

Excerpt Two – Parents from mainland China

1   Author: What has made you bring Shan over here to Britain?

2   Mum: We have learnt from books and TV that the British education system is excellent, especially famous for its individualised teaching.

3   Author: Did you have any idea about schools and teachers before you came over here?

4   Dad: We heard that English teachers were of high academic credentials, even primary teachers had a university degree.

5   Author: Then how much you know about school teachers in China?

6   Mum: Most of them have only graduated from two-year teachers' college, equivalent to sixth form colleges in Britain.

7   Dad: But the whole system is different from the British one, isn't it?

8   Author: Yes, the teacher training system in China can be understood as a multiple-tier structure, which has been modified on the lines of the former Soviet model since 1949. Within this structure, two-year normal schools for the training of Kindergarten teachers; two-year educational colleges for training primary school teachers; three-year teachers' colleges for the training of teachers in lower secondary schools; and four-year teachers' universities responsible for training teachers working in upper secondary schools.

9   Dad: In comparison, the English teachers' academic level is then ...

10   Mum: I heard they all had profound knowledge of child psychology and pedagogy.

11   Dad: Another advantage here is the size of each class, there are much fewer children in a class.

12   Mum: Chinese primary has got as big as over 50 pupils in a class, with one tutor and several subject teachers.

13 Dad: This makes it impossible for teachers to take care of individual differences.

14 Mum: We hope Shan will benefit from her English school here.

15 Dad: My initial thought was that since English was a global language, and we suffered from being poor in the language, why not let Shan have an opportunity to learn English in the native country?

16 Mum: At least, she will learn good English here, and return some day with a good command of fluent English.

It is apparent from the above excerpts that the Hong Kong family has their own beliefs and expectations about English education shaped by their own experiences in colonial education systems. Their reasons for migration are very practical: the couple want to find a job and make more money, the children want a less competitive but better valued education. Both husband and wife, from their own bitter past, particularly aspire for their daughters to be socially mobile and get into white-collar or professional jobs by getting educational qualifications, and English schools, less competitive in their eyes, are regarded as easier places where their children's life chances will be enhanced. This is the view shared by many migrants from former colonial countries.

While the Hong Kong couple came to realise the advantage of English schools directly from their former colonial reality, the mainland couple got to know Britain and the English education system through literature, media and their English experience abroad.

What is noticeable is that the mainland parents are keen on their daughter getting a good command of English and other broader knowledge, whereas the Hong Kong parents are more concerned about their daughters' opportunities to earn qualifications for better jobs in the future. The former are holding a more idealistic point of view while the latter are much more realistic. Also, we can see the different myths held by both families, with the mainland couple showing more interest in individualised teaching and the Hong Kong couple being keen on competition.

All these differences would have resulted in their different attitudes to schools and teachers: the parents from mainland China being keener to find out the reality in their daughter's school, and the parents from Hong Kong trusting that their daughters' education and prospects would be secured once they entered the UK.

The parents' concern for their children's present situation

Shan's parents show enthusiasm for English education, and are anxious about their daughter's progress in her new school. This attitude is linked to their knowledge and expectations, as discussed earlier. However, they are also keen to know what is going on in Shan's school and how they can contribute. They expect teachers to explain to them the school policy and their educational philosophy for children like Shan, who has recently arrived in this country with little English. The following conversation reveals the couples' complex feeling about their daughter's school and teachers.

Excerpt Three – Shan's parents

1	Author:	How long are you going to stay in this country?
2	Mum:	It depends on how well Shan learns English as we don't think there is a problem if we would like to stay on.
3	Dad:	It is really not easy for Shan. She has lots of difficulties in the class.
4	Author:	What did her teacher say?
5	Mum:	She didn't say anything really, but always asks us not to worry as kids would pick up language quickly.
6	Author:	Does Shan have any language support in the class?
7	Mum:	No, hardly any.
8	Author:	Did you have an opportunity to talk with the head teacher or other teachers?
9	Dad:	We did talk, but the head teacher said there was no extra teacher taking care of the support, as the school has only one learning support teacher, and she is too busy to take the job. He told us to be patient as well.
10	Mum:	We have no idea what is the school policy for children like Shan.
11	Dad:	At the moment, learning English is Shan's priority as it is the key to her other subject learning. If Shan cannot catch up in a short period, she is going to fail in many ways.
12	Mum:	We don't doubt that the British education is famous for its individualised teaching, but I just cannot see this from Shan's experience.
13	Dad:	Shan's encounter is quite out of our expectation.
14	Mum:	I have a feeling that teachers here seem quite carefree, they don't really bother if children learn, 'well done' is a common expression.

15 Dad: The encouragement is good but the point is to make sure that children in school should learn what they are supposed to learn.

16 Mum: This is why we cannot make a decision of how long we are going to stay in this country. What a big headache !

The Hong Kong couple are clearly interested in their children's education, even if they have not had much contact with schools and teachers, and know very little about the school. They are very eager to have someone who can speak both English and Cantonese as their go between. What impresses me most is that the mother, in particular, is very keen on the teachers' comment on their children. Their attitude to the school and teachers is well reflected in the excerpt below:

Excerpt Four – Mother of the two daughters

1 Author: Do Kapo and Wington like their school?

2 Mum: I think they are generally OK about the school.

3 Author: How about their school lesson? Do they understand the language?

4 Mum: I don't know much what is going on in school but I know they normally don't have homework after school.

5 Author: Don't you worry because the kids are too relaxed, or talk to their teacher about their special situation?

6 Mum: Yes, but what can I do about it since I don't speak English? And time is a big problem, I think.

7 Author: What do you mean by 'time'?

8 Mum: I mean if I ask some friends to contact the school for me but it is hard as they all work in the restaurant and by the time they finish working, the school is closed.

9 Author: What can I do for you if you like? I am very happy to.

10 Mum: I just want to know if my children can catch up with the class, but sometimes I say to myself that the school has its method, they will be fine soon and no need for me to worry.

11 Author: What did the children tell you about their teachers?

12 Mum: They all came back telling me their teachers were nice and said a lot of good things about them like 'brilliant', 'well done', etc. To be honest I feel good about it but I am not sure as well because I know they are very difficult at the moment and have to catch up quickly.

13   Author: What do you think can make them catch up quickly?

14   Mum: They have to study harder and ask for help whenever it is needed.

15   Author: Do you want me to speak to their class teachers and see if the school can offer some individual support ?

16   Mum: Yes, yes, it is very kind of you to do so (*eyes light up*). You see I cannot speak English myself, so what I can do is make sure my children are learning in the school. I always believe once kids are sent to schools, they will be educated anyway, otherwise what is point to have schools and teachers?

From the two excerpts above we read that both couples are preoccupied with children's English learning as they believe that language is the key to their subject learning in school. Both sets of parents are supportive of their children's schools. However, as they differ considerably in their knowledge of the English education system, their attitudes to schools and teachers are different.

The Hong Kong couple, especially the mother, expressed overall satisfaction with teachers and the school, and placed faith in the comments of the teachers. This is partly because she has just been released from the high pressure in Hong Kong, and partly because she has little knowledge of English schools but respects the professionalism of the teachers. Although she is concerned about whether her daughters are able to understand the lesson with limited English, she has no idea what to do to help them. She tends to accept the reality of the school, and demonstrate a greater reliance on teachers' opinions, and on what they were told about school arrangements for their daughters.

However, the mainland couple express more of their anxiety for their daughter's perceived disadvantages in the class. The mismatch of their expectations with what schools actually offer has made them think whether teachers' comments such as 'well done' or 'doing well' really count or they mean nothing tangible but are rather perfunctory. They become critical of what they see in school, and ready to make suggestions. From the present school policy for those newly arrived EAL children, they actually see the reference to individualised education and how the myth that Britain is famous for this dies hard.

The parents' responses to their children's disadvantages in schools

Driven by concern, if not anxiety, for their children's progress in the English schools, both the mainland couple and the Hong Kong couple are eager to help their children's education. However, due to their different attitudes based on their knowledge of English schools and teachers, what they can do for their children in terms of extra support (additional education provision) are not the same. The following discussion centres on different strategies developed in the two families as a response to the disadvantages faced by their children in the English mainstream school.

Shan's family is anxious about their daughter's inability to cope in the class-room. They themselves are also very involved in Shan's learning, for instance, the father looks for books, exercises and videos in bookshops, and learns new words and expressions with her every night. The mother checks anything brought back from the school, helps her out with the assignments given by the teacher, and signs the daybook when asked. They prepare a pocket English dictionary for Shan and check the words every weekend. They also ask her to recite lessons or dialogues from memory, and even try to speak English with her, though with a strong Chinese accent. The couple also help Shan to collect some useful information for her history, geography and science lessons. The parents, in order to minimise Shan's feeling of loneliness in her new school, send her to London Mandarin School, where she is able to meet her Mandarin-speaking friends and also share learning experiences with some older bilingual classmates. The diary below reflects how this self-help approach is being applied at home.

> *Tomorrow is Saturday again, but I have not much weekend to talk about as either my father or mother would have an English lesson with me. They use New Concept English, the textbook they used at university to help me learn English. The textbook is well written in English/Chinese, every lesson is followed by 'new words and expressions', 'notes on the text' and 'written exercises'. My mum asks me to memorise all the new words and expressions in each lesson, and checks if I know the spelling and the meaning well enough. My father even asks me to recite from memory the whole text and do some translations from English to Chinese and Chinese to English. Hard as it is, but I think it is worth doing. My parents, though, are not good at pronunciation and intonation; they are able to tell me most of the grammar rules and the usages. In order to get the sound right, I normally have them checked with my classmates. I find my English has improved better in this way.* (Translated passage from Shan's diary)

Shan's experience of family support has been shared by many other older children in London Mandarin School.

The Hong Kong couple, at first, were quite at ease about their daughters' new school. This stemmed, perhaps, from their limited knowledge about how English schools work, about the curriculum and the whole educational process. However, when they realised the importance of English language support for newcomers, they began to seek support elsewhere from outside the English schools, from the community school.

Although community schools are mostly set up for Chinese and cultural maintenance, Republic Chinese School where Kapo and Wington are going, has a class with a focus on teaching English to young adults. Kapo and Wington join in the class with permission from the class tutor. The English class taught in Cantonese works very well for the two sisters and they feel much more confident than before.

No doubt, the Hong Kong couple, though lacking knowledge of educational issues, have actually managed to supply their children with the best additional provision, which contributes to their daughters' survival in their education.

> Today I was late for my Chinese school as we were held up by the traffic. It is too bad as I don't want to miss my English class before we have my Chinese one. At the moment I am more concerned about learning English and catching up with my English classmates. This English class is for adults but my sister and I have just joined in with the head teacher's special permission. To be honest, there is not much fun in this class though, we learnt at least some basic knowledge of English, and the teacher, Mr Feng, can speak both English and Cantonese, which helps us a lot more in learning. I know my sister felt bored sometimes in the lesson as she is a bit too young for this class, but it is ok for me as I can't expect anything better in the present situation. I know some of my father's friends even pay £20 per hour for their children's one to one extra lessons, but my parents cannot afford that for us. However I feel lucky enough to be in this class. (Translated passage from Kapo's diary)

Apparently Kapo has had very positive comments about their parents' home support and appreciated what has been provided for English support in her community school. Like many other parents from poor educational backgrounds, the Hong Kong parents cannot involve themselves in actual work with children, but their provision of extra tuition for children in the weekend community school has benefited their children. What is noticeable from Kapo's diary above is that she mentions the fact that many Chinese parents pay for children's individual tuition outside the school. Actually this is quite common among Chinese parents, regardless of different linguistic and educational backgrounds.

The role of Chinese community schools and many ways of enrichment

Despite the fact that Chinese community schools are diverse in many ways, the aims of the two Chinese schools – London Mandarin and Republic Chinese – are quite similar. They aim to:

1. Provide Chinese language teaching for overseas Chinese children.

2. Educate children about Chinese culture and history.

3. Pass on to the younger generation various aspects of Chinese morality and a sense of identity.

4. Bridge the gap between parents and their children in communication as well as in views and beliefs.

5. Supplement mainstream schooling by providing extra lessons on various core subjects (English Maths and Science) at GCSE and A level.

These five objectives indicate that Chinese community schools in general place a strong emphasis on the transmission of the Chinese language and culture, and on the provision of an additional source of learning via formal teaching and other informal extra-curricular-activities, for example, singing, dancing, orchestra, table-tennis, badminton, Chinese chess, martial arts and traditional festivals. It is not a segregated education but a complementary form of schooling to meet the various expectations of Chinese parents in Britain. Thus, in the children's eyes, the Chinese school is an extending school, where their bilinguality will be enhanced, and they will learn many things that are not available in the English school, and at the same time contribute to their overall academic development. The following comments from five older bilingual students in a student workshop reflect what they have learnt from the Chinese community school and how the Chinese culture, language and methodology help in their way to success.

Knowledge and skills

I was born in China but I moved to England with my parents at 5. When I was 10 my parents sent me to the Chinese community school to learn Chinese literacy skills though I am able to talk fluently at home. The class starts at 12:00 with lesson of Chinese general knowledge, and is then followed by three periods of language education till 4.00. After that there is a wide range of optional courses to attract our interest, for instance, chess club, calligraphy group, dancing class, Chinese painting lesson, Kung fu workshop, etc are very popular among both parents and students. We normally finish school at 5. I think all these activities encourage us to adopt a more balanced attitude toward our learning. (*Ying Ma*)

I began my Chinese schooling at home and then joined the weekend school for more activities. Recently I have moved to this Sunday Chinese School because they provide GCSE courses not only for the Chinese language, but for maths and science revision as well. Teachers are researchers themselves at the university in London and parents as well. So they know very well both the subject and the test requirement, thus very helpful to us. (*Susan Wu*)

At that time I was often teased and pushed around by some classmates simply because I was not yet fluent in English. I was often seen as an easy target and also wronged by teachers in the school because I have no way to defend myself. Later I was recommended by a friend of my mum's to this London Mandarin School where I could learn English from a bilingual teacher and make friends with my classmates who share with me the same learning experience. I am now in the Chinese A level class, but to be honest with you, at that time I came to the Chinese school not for the development of Chinese like many others do but only for my EAL support. (*Joe Lin*)

Attitudes and commitment

Our Chinese lessons have taught us to 'work hard and aim high', which has manifested itself in many Chinese parents abroad. Ambitions provide us with motivation and a hard working attitude which is applied of our own accord. Laziness and inefficiency are thus perceived as barriers to progress. This dedication has evolved into a routine of early revision resulting in better grades. This sense of self-motivation is encouraged by parents who see education as being of paramount importance to a child's development. (*Nicola Xiang*)

We have learnt to be independent in our learning and develop as well a sense of self-discipline and responsibility towards our work, with the commitment involved in weekly lessons as well as daily homework tasks being quite substantial but completed well before the deadline. Work isn't seen as a chore, rather as a pathway to better future. The social and academic support given by Chinese Schools is proving to be central in our education and the adopted attitudes towards learning shown in the Chinese lessons have been vital to the academic success. (*Joyce Chen*)

Sense of Chinese identity and cultural heritages

'Chinese and the Chinese' are closely linked like 'English and the English', 'French and the French'. The same spelling embodies both language and nationality, which means if you don't know the Chinese language and you are not counted as a proper Chinese. Therefore, studying Chinese is part of our heritage and there is an added motivation to do well if we have an innate sense of identity developed through the language learning. The Chinese school has allowed us to interact with other people our age who share our culture and linguistic background. (*Joe Lin*)

Confucianism is one of important cultural heritages shared by all Chinese regardless of different political ideologies and different regions and dialects. Literacy training is seen as the way led to 'status mobility' and social economic advancement. The way in which Chinese school students view their own academic achievements are inevitably influenced by such heritage. Healthy competition is of course promoted under the Confucian heritage culture, which proves further motivation for both parents and students alike. (*Ying Ma*)

Methodology and forms of learning

'Chinese' attitude towards education has resulted in rigorous yet effective learning strategies. These have proven themselves to be highly successful in providing students with the resources to achieve the highest standards, whilst also encouraging development of the well-rounded individual. Moreover, in our Chinese lesson, English is valued for comprehension purpose and bilingual application. Content and language integrated learning are encouraged, and through back and forth translation practice, our bilingual capacity has been improved. (*Nicola Xiang*)

Chinese being a character based language stimulates a different area of brain activity to when English is being used, so this may have a positive influence on our capacity to reason in different ways and to consider a question from different angles. (*Susan Wu*)

Reciting and memorising words and facts play a large part in the Chinese education system; however it is coupled with understanding, logical reasoning and application of knowledge rather than just regurgitating facts. Our Chinese lessons at the London Mandarin School have taught us to combine a creative approach and self-discovery that enable us to utilise a variety of approaches creating greater flexibility and ultimately academic success. (*Joyce Chen*)

The above comments indicate the many diverse benefits that such complementary schooling has brought for our children. It has been demonstrated that Chinese community schools play a very important role in their children's educational success through their function of language and culture maintenance, construction of Chinese identity, as well as supplementing mainstream education. They also serve as a bridge between parents and children, between two languages and cultures.

Conclusion

This study demonstrates that parental involvement improves children's educational performance, that the involvement manifest in active interest, constant encouragement and high expectations has been the most valuable driving factor. The Chinese parents, regardless of different educational backgrounds and different occupations, mostly share high expectations about education and also high aspirations for their children. They are a powerful influence on the children's academic development.

Although they differ in their strategies due to their individual experiences and knowledge, they are all active supporters of their children's education. Those better off parents provide not only a good learning environment but also resources to invest in their children's learning. The better educated parents are able to provide direct teaching or look for reference materials in bookshops and libraries, or even buy them in China. The poor and less educated parents, though unable to provide their children with practical help or afford extra tuition after school, can still support their children through the community and the weekend schools.

All this has been evident in our investigation into two families of recent arrivals. What needs to be specially recognised is the poor parents' tremendous efforts to combat socioeconomic hardship and the many educational disadvantages that their children have faced in and out of school. Families have suffered considerable socioeconomic hardship and the older generations have often had little formal education either in mainland China, Hong Kong or the UK, yet their children have largely succeeded. Those children's achievement is particularly significant in the face of continuing disadvantages (Tomlinson, 2000), racial discrimination in the education system (Pang, 1999), and new forms of inequality based on problematic inclusion issues in the mainstream classroom that three newly arrived girls have experienced (Chen, 2007). It is, therefore, crucially important for educators to find out what might enable these students to achieve such results in order to inform work with other minority groups in schools.

Moreover, when Chinese children have been hailed as high achievers, the difficulties and inequalities they face in the first place should not be glossed over. The story of the vast majority of Chinese high achievers should not become a myth that diverts our attention from the problems that many Chinese are still experiencing, for example, the sociocultural barriers, language differences, and socioeconomic factors. Neither should we be prevented from unravelling the educational inequalities that those parents encounter (Li, 2003; Olsen, 1997). In fact, the Chinese as a group face both discrimination and problems accessing public and social services (Chau and Yu, 2001; Cheng and Heath, 1993).

The image of Chinese parents as docile and non-confrontational (Chun, 1995) and the least assimilated of all minority groups (Watson, 1977) has been conceptualised stereotypically. Any paternalistic positioning of the Chinese firstly as an economically successful silent community and, secondly, as a model minority which has achieved academic success, is based on ill-conceived stereotypes of the Chinese as 'collectivist, conformist, entrepreneurial, deferent, and sticking to conventions' (Parker, 2000 and Chau and Yu, 2001). These perceptions are reflected in some accounts (Sham and Woodrow, 1998) of the Chinese approach to learning.

In fact, the high value placed on education by the Chinese in Britain is one of most important factors that contribute to their educational achievement, and this, coupled with respect for elders which allows the transmission of strong values from parents to children, is found rooted in the Chinese cultural heritage in terms of Confucian ideology. This ideology, as a symbol of Chinese cultural identity, has never been destroyed by any foreign invasion, even during the period of colonial Hong Kong before 1997.

Such a strong national faith in Confucianism explains why Chinese people value education so highly, and this has positive effects both on Chinese children's educational success in the British education system and on their future development in society.

Research data also indicate that Chinese community schools are highly valued by Chinese parents and children alike. Such schooling plays a pivotal role in the transmission of Chinese language and culture (Francis and Archer, 2005). In this sense, parents and many children portray their Chinese school as an important resource contributing to their ethnic and cultural identity as well as their academic success, where a Chinese attitude towards education does not mean anything segregated from or hostile to mainstream education but serves as a catalyst to minimise conflicts and supplement mainstream education. Chinese parents feel strongly that only through knowledge of the language, and thereby history and literature, can the children have a true understanding of their parents' attitudes, standards and values.

Some conflicts are inevitable in the family, though it is hoped that Chinese community schools eliminate conflicts between Chinese parents and their children. One issue that needs to be clarified is that, unlike Caribbean parents who have been, justifiably, highly critical of English culture and the English education system in terms of offering their children equality of opportunity, Chinese parents have not suffered in the same way. They have chosen to set up schools to maintain their language and cultural identity, not as a response to dissatisfaction with the English education system. Chinese children choose to prove themselves by working hard, respecting teachers and being tolerant of different opinions.

In short, it is those factors manifest in active parental involvement as well as in the diverse benefits of complementary schooling that have contributed significantly to Chinese children's generally high educational achievement. It is hoped that the findings in this study will serve as an important reference for policy improvements that might take place in future.

5

Learning Portuguese:
a tale of two worlds

Olga Barradas

Introduction

This chapter tells the tale of two worlds, of Portuguese children in Portuguese language classes and in English mainstream schools. It is based on a research project that analysed national and local achievement data of Portuguese pupils in London and compared the academic results of pupils who attended Portuguese classes with other Portuguese pupils from the same mainstream English schools who did not. Parent and pupil interviews were also included and these gave valuable insights into the families' perceptions and feelings about the role of Portuguese classes in their children's lives.

The chapter begins with a brief historical overview of Portuguese classes in south London and illustrates this with excerpts of interview data. The second part develops a rationale for attending Portuguese language classes by examining some key research studies. The third part presents the key findings from the research study and shows the benefits of attending Portuguese classes. The chapter concludes by asking new questions about the place of community languages in mainstream schools as the Key Stage Two Framework for Languages begins to make an impact across England. It also questions the extent to which community language classes are able to benefit from new technologies and argues that we have reached a point where the 'one model fits all' strategy no longer applies. There is now a need to respond to a changing political and socio-economic reality by developing new approaches that befit the communities' diverse needs and interests today.

A brief historical overview of Portuguese classes

We cannot say exactly when Portuguese classes in the UK were started but they have certainly existed for almost as long as the Portuguese community has been established. Initially, during the 1960s, they were organised by the migrants' associations and community groups in the London area as part of their cultural activities. Strong parental involvement was certainly a feature of these classes. The teachers were recruited locally and the classes took place in the church halls and other buildings that were available to these community groups. This meant that everything had to be paid for by the parents, including the books and materials used by the children as well as recruiting and paying for the teachers.

In Portugal this was a time of economic and political difficulties. Although some signs of struggle could be seen, the dictatorship that had been ruling since 1928 was still strongly entrenched. Colonial war had erupted in the, then, Portuguese African colonies and the number of people leaving the country for economic reasons was augmented by those who came to escape from the secret state police and military conscription. By 1975, one year after the revolution that restored the country to democratic government, the number of Portuguese people living in the UK was estimated to be around 4000 people (SOPEMI Report, 1976). In 1981 Reid *et al* (1985) estimated the Portuguese community to number around 30,000. By then, under the umbrella of the Greater London Council, Portuguese community classes were already taking place after school hours in a Westminster school. Nevertheless, the teachers in these classes continued to be paid by the parents. It was only in 1976 that the Portuguese government through its Ministry of Education took responsibility for the recruitment of teachers and organisation of Portuguese classes abroad, generally known as Portuguese Language and Culture (PLC) classes.

At an international level, several socio-economic as well as political factors drew attention to the situation of migrant workers. This enabled the Portuguese government to profit from European support. Under the influence of an EEC Directive (European Economic Council, 1977) the Portuguese were able to obtain endorsement from foreign governments. In practical terms this meant that financial help was received from the British education authorities with regard to the hiring of school classrooms. On the other hand, in the UK, the entrance of foreign workers into the country was strictly controlled. This control continued until 1986 when Portugal joined the then European Economic Community (EEC). The official stance contributed to the creation of a closed group identity by the Portuguese community members, an identity that kept them separate from the mainstream throughout the 1970s and early 1980s. As Ana's father – one of the parents involved in the research project – tells us below, the message that was perceived by the migrants themselves was of 'otherness', of distrust rather than acceptance, and inferiority rather than diversity. Unless individual reference is given, all graphs and texts quoted have been extracted from Barradas, (2004):

> When you got here, you were like a prisoner. The first four years when I came here, as you left the airport you already had to say what was your door's number. The police had already given me a book with a stamp saying you are going to such door... And if I moved from this door to next door, you had to go to the police and take that book to write again that you had moved to such door, do you understand? And work, six months, you were forced to stay for six months in that job, without changing work, otherwise you would go back to Portugal. Whether you liked it or not you had to stay there for six months... And we were forced to always carry that book in the pocket... [You couldn't] talk back in those days, not to open your mouth to anything. It was like being a prisoner. During those four years, I felt somewhat... how do I say it? I felt tranquil because I had plenty to eat and drink, to tell the truth, but I really felt like a prisoner. Detained. That's why I was looking forward to those four years to go, to be free, as the English say, free. (Ana's father)

The PLC classes focused mainly on literacy skills in the mother tongue. For the children to read and write in their first language had been the main objective for all parents, who intended to return to the country of origin. In this case, the Portuguese government expected that its citizens in the diaspora, who were contributing with significant amounts of foreign currency to the national economy, would return home as soon as the political and economic situation improved. At that time the significant financial investment in Portugal of its citizens abroad signalled their intention to do so. So it was as a duty to its citizens that the right for children of Portuguese communities abroad to receive education in this language was enshrined in the National Constitution. Both the Portuguese authorities and the migrants themselves expected the period of residence abroad to be temporary and transitional. Given that the main goal of these families was to return to their place of origin, it was crucial that their children would be able to integrate into the Portuguese school system upon return. This led to a curriculum being created in the late 1970s for the PLC classes that closely followed those taught in Portugal in both style and content. This curriculum focused on Portuguese language and literacy, history and geography, ie regional characteristics, physical and social aspects as well as traditions at both primary and secondary school level.

Having the classes organised and run by the Portuguese Ministry of Education had both positive and negative aspects. On the one hand, it offered parents the peace of mind of not having to worry about the organisational and financial problems normally associated with this type of education. It not only represented stability and continuity but also offered a guarantee of teaching quality. All teachers recruited by the Ministry were fully qualified, both those recruited in Portugal and those recruited locally. On the other hand, having a central model imposed on each country meant that it might not correspond to the real and changing needs of the community.

A clear example of this can be found in the PLC classes' curriculum which prescribed oracy – but not literacy – during the first school year. This practice has remained in place until recently. While in other European countries it may have been feasible to conceive of a situation where children in their first year of attending Portuguese classes need to focus solely on the development of oracy skills, for the children in this country that would not be advisable. In the UK children start attending PLC classes from the age of seven. However, most have attended formal schooling from at least the age of five and their literacy skills in English are already developing. It simply would not make sense to keep them away from literacy in Portuguese during that initial year.

At the time of writing, a new official document providing a model for the teaching of Portuguese abroad is under testing. This document – *Quadro de Referência para o Ensino Português no Estrangeiro* (QuaREPE) (DGIDC, 2005) – is based amongst other reference documents on the Common European Framework and it constitutes the setting upon which all Portuguese Teaching Abroad – *Ensino Português no Estrangeiro* (EPE) – will be based. It is described as offering a global model, organised according to five competence levels, with profile descriptors by component (oral understanding, reading, oral production/interaction, written production/interaction). It purports to attain the full recognition, validation and certification of Portuguese teaching abroad, whilst promoting co-operation between education systems and participants in the education process.

Although the aim of obtaining recognition for the students' linguistic skills using an instrument comparable between education systems is a laudable one, it remains unclear how such an instrument will adequately measure the attainment of children such as those who took part in the study described later in this chapter. Given that its focus, judging by the descriptors given, appears to be the development of a Second or Foreign Language, the linguistic achievement of children speaking Portuguese as a community language and often as a mother tongue, may show great variations. The same child may show a high level of competence in oracy and a low level of written skills.

More interesting, however, will be the interplay between language *per se* and its use in a particular social context. It is possible that some examples of language use will be mistaken for linguistic miscues or errors when the characteristics of a community are ignored (see, for example, Mayone-Dias, 1986; Keating, 1990; Barradas, 1993; Barradas, 1996). It is through the skills and professional experience of the teachers that potential maladjustments between the policies and real life situations can be avoided. Indeed, teaching community language classes requires not only a knowledge of the language and a multidisciplinary subject content but also an awareness of the needs and expectations of pupils as individuals and as part of an evolving community.

An analysis of the *circa* 3000 pupils who attend PLC classes nowadays would reveal a range of language abilities encompassing the native-like as well as those for whom Portuguese is a language that their grandparents speak at home, reflecting the diversity of the Portuguese community in this country. Nevertheless, parents continue to try to pass on the linguistic heritage to their children. As Carlos' mother – another parent involved in the research study – explains, in a society where carers outside the family take on the role previously played by grandparents, this is increasingly difficult:

> Oh! I think that it is very important that a person put their children to learn Portuguese, because many Portuguese children cannot speak Portuguese. Especially those that were born here. The parents have to work, and they have to leave their children with minders and normally, those are people that speak in English to them. Of course, the children will begin to learn the English language, not the Portuguese. Although they speak Portuguese at home, but it is so little. It is not enough to learn. And I think it is very important that the children go to school to learn... Of course, to continue speaking our language. I think it is important that our children learn the same language as their parents. For me, I think that is very important because – it is a very beautiful language. (Carlos' mother)

As the Portuguese community continues to grow – estimated at the time of writing to exceed 350,000 in the UK – community members now include a proportion of second generation, and in much reduced numbers a third generation is also emerging. At the same time, attracted by the offer of employment, large numbers of Portuguese people continue to arrive in this country. New communities of Portuguese speakers continue to emerge all over the UK and Portuguese beginner learners of English as an additional language (EAL) join schools throughout the country.

Despite over 30 years having passed since the beginning of Portuguese teaching in the UK, there is still no Portuguese school. Unlike other communities who have managed to create their own schools, either by setting up private institutions or voluntary-aided schools, Portuguese classes continue to take place in classrooms hired by the hour and to be the sole responsibility of the Portuguese Government. In terms of organisation, they continue to take place after school hours, usually between 4.00 and 8.00 in the evening. In the 2004-2005 school year, they took place in 40 different schools in and outside London and 34 Portuguese teachers taught PLC classes to 2550 students, usually organised in groups of between 10 and 20 students, in two weekly sessions of around 1.5 hours per week (IGE, 2005). However, despite sharing premises, there continues to be a rift between what goes on in the evening and in the mainstream classroom.

A while ago, reflecting on my experiences as a mother tongue teacher, I wrote:

> I began teaching Portuguese in London in 1986... Like my Portuguese colleagues, I felt the gulf between us and the English classroom teachers. It was as if the '4 o'clock watershed' made me invisible. Most English teachers had no idea of what was going on, what we were doing, how we were working. Some did not know that the children were taking part in evening classes in that same school. Many were quite concerned that the children were overworked which could be detrimental to their progress, therefore suggesting to the parents that they should avoid sending their children to evening classes. It was also common for parents to be advised to speak only in English at home. As time went by, parents felt more at ease talking to me and would sometimes ask, especially those with younger children, whether I thought speaking Portuguese at home would actually hinder their development. (Barradas, 2004)

In that respect, little seems to have changed in the past thirty years. Portuguese teachers remain (almost) invisible in their after-hours work. Given this scenario, one could be forgiven for having doubts regarding the long-term prospect of these classes. Yet, the continued growth of the community would imply a greater involvement with schools and social visibility. One would expect the language needs of Portuguese students to be taken into account, not just in terms of having English as an additional language (EAL) but, more importantly, learning through their mother tongue as well as maintaining the development of that language.

But how can the linguistic needs of these students be provided for if officially there is no national record of their numbers? Despite local authorities having the possibility of collecting the numbers of Portuguese speakers in their schools, that information is not available centrally. On a national basis, Portuguese students continue to be included in the broad category of 'Any Other White Background'.

Although official guidance points towards acknowledging children's cultural and linguistic backgrounds in the classroom (see for example *Standards for Qualified Teacher Status* (TTA, 2003)), this does not correspond to teaching in the child's language. The onus of providing education in the child's first language is still on parental organisations and initiatives. In the case of the Portuguese children, there are also notable exceptions where Portuguese teachers work in the mainstream supporting the development of these students. But this kind of EAL support – where the use of Portuguese functions as a transitional aid – is only used until the students develop the necessary linguistic skills in English to survive in the classroom. There is no evidence that academic work in the mother tongue will continue after the children achieve a good command of English. Thus, the development of academic skills in and through the medium of mother tongue remains in the realm of after-school classes.

Why attend PLC classes?

There is evidence both from this country and from abroad to show that there are advantages in teaching children through their mother tongue. In Canada and in the US, where until recently various types of bilingual or dual-language education programmes were available, researchers have demonstrated clearly the added value that this type of education brings about for children learning English as an additional language. In the US, bilingual children who have had the chance to attend longer bilingual education programmes (late exit) obtained academic results closer to those students in the general population than the children who left bilingual programmes earlier (Ramírez, 1992; Beykont, 1994).

In the Netherlands, work with Turkish nursery school children suggests that, if there is opportunity and motivation to develop literacy skills in two languages, these skills will be transferred between both languages. Verhoeven (1991) found that literacy skills being developed in one language strongly predict corresponding skills in another language acquired later in time. There is also strong evidence to support the view proposed by Cummins (1984) that to develop the type of language required for achieving academic success in a second or additional language takes five to seven years.

A long-term study investigating the achievement of more than 700,000 students in the US also pointed out the need for continued support in the students' mother tongue (Thomas and Collier, 1997). The authors concluded that the students schooled totally in English, who arrived in the US between the ages of 8 and 11, and who had received at least two to five years of schooling through their mother tongue in their home country, were the lucky ones who took only five to seven years to reach levels of academic achievement typical of native speakers. Those who arrived before the age of 8 required seven to ten years or more.

Students who arrived after the age of 12 and had formal schooling in their country of origin, were making steady gains with each year of school but by the end of high school, they had run out of time to catch up academically with their peers. Moreover, as students progress quickly in conversational language in their first school years (Cummins 1979, 1980), teachers can be misled into assuming that this rate of progress will continue. Nevertheless, these students tend to fall behind the typical achievement levels of native English speakers, resulting in a very significant, cumulative achievement gap by the end of their schooling (Thomas and Collier, 2002).

These authors all highlight the need for the continued development of the child's linguistic skills in the mother tongue and its link with academic and cognitive development. To achieve this, however, requires a dramatic change in our sociocultural environment. Bilingual education in this country has been the domain of private schools and experimental projects. With the exception of bilingual assistants and Ethnic Minority Achievement (EMA) and EAL support, there is no Portuguese teaching within mainstream education.

In this situation then, is there an advantage for Portuguese students in attending PLC classes? After all, in these classes they are taught in Portuguese about topic areas that have no direct impact on the English school curriculum, and for example there is no teaching in English, Maths or Science. Can PLC classes contribute to children's development in the mainstream curriculum? Will the school performance of the children attending Portuguese classes be any different from those not attending?

Researching Portuguese classes

At the time of the study I will describe (Barradas, 2004) it seemed to be a *fait accompli* in local schools' hearsay that Portuguese students, as a group, had poor academic results. This was confirmed by the data published by Lambeth Education (2000), the only borough that published the school results of Portuguese students as a group. These students fared well below the local and national averages as measured by the standardised national tests, or SATs as they are often known. This result was pervasive across all Key Stages. Later information from other Local Education Authorities also appeared to indicate low achievement (Abreu and Lambert, 2003).

The only way to find out if there was, indeed, an advantage for Portuguese students in attending PLC classes would be to compare the academic results of those children attending the classes with other Portuguese children from the same schools who did not attend. Nevertheless, such a comparison, undoubtedly important, did not explain why parents made the effort to accompany their children through many years of evening classes. Surely, there had to be a stronger motive than just being able to communicate in Portuguese or to achieve a GCSE in this language. After all, many children who do not attend PLC classes can express themselves well in Portuguese and there is no requirement to attend classes in order to sit for the exam.

The study was conducted in a low socio-economic area of south London and considered the opinions of a group of parents and schoolchildren as well as comparing the end of Key Stage results for 166 children from ages 7 to 16. In order to obtain comparable groups, the data for both groups of children attending and not attending PLC classes were collected from the same schools in the same area.

The academic results obtained in mainstream education indicated a considerable difference between the two groups of children in terms of their end of Key Stage results. In the work done by Thomas and Collier (2002), mentioned above, those students who had not received continued support in their mother tongue fell significantly behind the typical achievement levels of native English speakers at the end of their schooling. Yet here, although differences could be found throughout the four key stages, they were already markedly visible in Key Stage One. At the age of 7, the children attending PLC classes achieved results in reading, writing and mathematics that were comparable to both the local and national averages. In the writing test and particularly in mathematics tests, their results exceeded the local average.

The results of the students not attending these classes, on the other hand, fell behind all the other averages (see Table One). It is noteworthy that most children at the end of Key Stage One will have attended mother tongue (PLC) classes for only one year. Although these classes have a strong focus on reading (particularly reading comprehension) and writing skills, there is no input in mathematics.

The results achieved in this key stage could, therefore, also reflect the high input from the parents in the early ages, helping at home in Portuguese with homework and teaching the basic skills to their children. Nonetheless, there was no evidence to suggest that the same did not happen with the other children. This could be taken as an indication that the children attending mother tongue classes may be advantaged in their use of academic language and may be more familiar with the linguistic requirements both of formal learning and of assessment situations.

Table 1: Percentage of students attaining level two or above

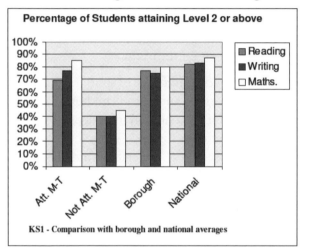

In Key Stages Two and Three, the differences between the groups were not as marked, although the students attending mother tongue classes continued to show an advantage. In Key Stage Three, the children not attending PLC classes showed the effect of schooling and were beginning to catch up with those who attended the classes. Nevertheless, there was still a tendency for the group attending mother tongue classes to achieve higher results than the group not attending. This was the case, in particular, for the writing part of the English test, to which the metalinguistic knowledge acquired in their literacy learning in Portuguese certainly contributed. In the English test (as a whole) 67% of the children attending PLC classes attained Level four or above, against 55% of the children not attending.

In Key Stage Three, despite students attending PLC classes having achieved results in English and Science that were close to those attained in the borough, these results were still well below the national average. Students not attending mother tongue classes, on the other hand, achieved below the local average on all three areas of assessment (English, Maths and Science). Interestingly, the students who attended PLC classes continued to demonstrate a significant advantage with regard to their counterparts not attending the classes. In the English test, 35% of the students attending PLC classes achieved Level five or above, against only 26% of the students in the non-attending group.

It would, thus, appear that the children attending PLC classes show an advantage in their early years that they maintain throughout their academic career. It is, however, in Key Stage Four that this advantage becomes particularly clear (see Table 2). At the end of compulsory education, the students who had attended PLC classes had overtaken those in the other group by a wide margin. A proportion of 41% of the students attending Portuguese classes attained five or more A*-C GCSEs. However, that number did not include the results obtained in the Portuguese exam. If these were added, the disparity would grow even wider as 64% of the students attending mother tongue classes achieved a result of either A or A* in their Portuguese GCSE.

Table 2: Percentage of pupils attaining five or more GCSEs

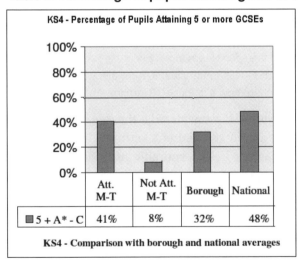

KS4 - Percentage of Pupils Attaining 5 or more GCSEs

	Att. M-T	Not Att. M-T	Borough	National
■ 5 + A* - C	41%	8%	32%	48%

KS4 - Comparison with borough and national averages

It is clear that there is a very tangible payoff for those who invest in mother tongue classes. Yet, how can we justify these striking differences in the results? It is likely that these classes' emphasis on literacy, on text decoding strategies, and on metalinguistic knowledge and skills, allows for the development of academic skills that will directly improve the school performance of these students. And, in line with what Cummins (2000) and other researchers (see, for example, Verhoeven, 1991; Ramírez, 1992 and Beykont, 1994) have proposed for bilingual programmes, PLC classes will also give them the tools to transfer knowledge and learning strategies to other contexts and educational situations. Sneddon's (2000a), Parke *et al*'s (2002) and Robertson's (2004) work, amongst others, has shown how children's metalinguistic awareness and strategies to negotiate meaning in community schools can be transferred to mainstream learning. By having a different cultural perspective on the way that the topics are approached, PLC lessons may also contribute to the development of analytic skills.

Furthermore, as the manuals used in the PLC classes are those published and used in mainstream education in Portugal, the texts they contain provide age appropriate literacy materials. At the same time as their linguistic skills are developed in a classroom context and shaped towards appropriate use in academic settings, the discussion and analysis of the content in the materials used will promote cognitive development. The students are forced to use higher level skills not only to identify information in a given text but also to explain, hypothesise, question and justify events and opinions. It is to this transfer of skills and knowledge that one of the pupils who was involved in the study, alludes when she says:

> When I go to the English school and I have something to do that I have done in the Portuguese school, then it is easy! All I have to do is translate it! ... (People who don't go to Portuguese classes) they don't learn more. Because, like this, they could know something. All they had to do was to translate it. And, this way, they have to use their head and ask the teachers how it is [done]. (Carmina, Year Six)

Another critical element that needs to be considered is the role of parents and other members of the extended family in children's learning. It has been reported that students whose parents held favourable attitudes toward bilingual education made faster progress in both English and Spanish and that bilingual work promoted parental involvement (Ramírez, 1992; Beykont, 1994). Gregory *et al* (2004) have shown how siblings can be competent teachers, relating in play to their younger brothers and sisters the knowledge they have acquired at school. They fine tune the strategies observed both at mainstream and community schools in order to create learning situations that are advantageous for all involved (Gregory and Williams, 2000; Gregory, 2001) Similarly, in another study that examined young children's multilingual literacies, Kenner notes:

> Joint activity with adults – parents, grandparents, aunts and uncles – clearly stimulated the children's literacy learning. It also gave opportunities for older siblings to observe teaching in action, helping them to develop knowledge and strategies as they themselves assumed a teaching role. (Kenner, 2004b:136)

The parents of the children attending Portuguese classes also brought other important factors to the equation. They made comments like *'If I were to go back in time, I tell you, I would study. I would study. Today, without a course [a qualification], you don't earn anything.'* (Silvia's father) and *'I did not have the possibility of study. He has that possibility. He can use it better'* (Filipe's mother).

These comments reflect an awareness of the importance that this society attributes to academic attainment. These parents were conscious of the social and economic disadvantage that their limited academic qualifications imposed on them and, as a consequence, had greater academic expectations for their children (Barradas, 2004). They were aware of the hostile environment regarding the maintenance and promotion of their children's bilingual skills.

They purposefully insisted on the development of Portuguese literacy and were resilient to the influences to discard their native language. In so doing, the parents in the group attending Portuguese classes were effectively involved in their children's learning and contributed to a strong cultural identity. To them, contributing to the development of a strong Portuguese facet in their child's life is clearly determined and part of their duty as parents. For Debbie's mother, it is as much her duty to ensure her daughter attends mainstream education as the Portuguese classes. Both constitute substantial components in Debbie's development:

> Debbie has already asked me: 'Mum, why do I always have to go to Portuguese school?' when she started liking the English school more. And I said 'because your father is Portuguese, you are Portuguese, and *you are* Portuguese.' And one day, one day you never know what will come until that day comes. One day you may need the Portuguese, and knowledge does not take up space, knowledge is never too much, as my grandmother used to say. (Debbie's mother)

A new dawn for Portuguese?

The role of linguistic identity as part of one's cultural and individual identity is recognised by the DfES when it acknowledges that language *'lies at the heart of ideas about individual identity and community'* (DfES, 2005b:4). The Key Stage Two Framework for Languages is designed to underpin the ambition set out in the National Languages Strategy that: *'Every child should have the opportunity throughout Key Stage 2 to study a foreign language and develop their interest in the culture of other nations'* (DfES, 2005a:47). In the document, the guidance given to those involved in selecting the languages to be taught at school has been worded to include the possibility of choosing a community language: *Schools are free to teach any modern foreign or community language* (DfES, 2005a:23). This, however, poses some difficulties. If children are to be entitled to learn a new language, how will learning their own community language correspond to that entitlement? Besides, if the children can continue to develop their mother tongue outside school, the parents themselves may feel that having their language taught within the mainstream becomes a limitation as it will reduce their choice of languages. Furthermore, given the prestige that certain European languages hold and the corresponding availability of teaching resources, schools will feel tempted to take the easier route.

Community language schools constitute a valuable resource already set up that could be used to link mainstream schools and the communities they serve effectively. Nevertheless, they are overlooked in the Framework Guidance. The closest this document comes to mentioning them is in the possible contribution to the teaching of languages in primary schools of:

- a foreign national without formal teaching qualifications who lives in the school's vicinity (working alongside a class teacher)

- other volunteers (such as parents) who happen to have languages expertise (working alongside a class teacher). (DfES, 2005a:19).

A formal link between community language teachers and mainstream schools would provide the former with recognition of their role as partners in bilingual children's education. Mainstream schools would have access to staff, fully qualified in the case of the Portuguese teachers, able to provide differentiation in the language teaching and competent in intercultural knowledge.

As Moore (1999) suggests, the full inclusion of bilingual children in society implies the development of sophisticated reading and writing skills, helping students to become functionally and culturally literate in more than one language and empowering them to challenge the *status quo*. The only possible way to do so is, evidently, through links with the community and the allocation of adequate resources. However, funding is a major problem for community language schools. Society continues to reap the benefits they offer but is reluctant to pay for their teachers' time or professional development. The investment, both in terms of time and finance, continues to be left to the individuals who organise and teach those classes as well as the parents or, such as in the case of PLC classes, to foreign governments.

Apart from the financial demands that implementing community language teaching poses to the communities, one point that can be overlooked is the availability and access to modern technologies. For Barrantes (2005):

> The digital divide constitutes a new challenge which faces the international community and threatens to further deepen the development disparities existing between the developed and developing countries. These disparities are unprecedented in humanity's history, especially as regards the new forms of exclusion and marginalization posed by the digital illiteracy.

In a digital age, the use of online resources is an essential part of the teaching and learning process. At a European level, this fact is reflected in the e-Europe 2005 action plan, e-Learning action plan and the e-Learning Programme to combat digital illiteracy and to promote virtual campuses and virtual twinning of schools.

In Portugal, *Escola Virtual*, an e-learning initiative supported by the government, has been set up to help children access educational resources online. Apart from resources for students in Portuguese mainstream education, this site also includes a section with resources for children learning/speaking Portuguese in other countries. Given the importance of digital technologies, these are important projects aimed at the younger generations but they have implications for linguistic minorities. How can parents be part of this digital world when their knowledge of English and use of Information and Communication Technologies (ICT) is limited?

This lack of ICT skills and knowledge constitutes digital illiteracy and prevents access to technological and online resources in society. Parents will depend on their children to access the new forms of information. In a way, this is reminiscent of a situation that leads to role-reversal between generations where, unless the use of an interpreter is available, parents depend on their children to access information and carry out tasks in everyday life. Not only does this constitute a form of social exclusion but, as some authors have put it, digital poverty.

Computers and digital equipment have become an essential tool in our life. In mainstream classrooms this is taken into account through the teaching of ICT skills to students and use of newer forms of technology such as the interactive white board. Yet, how many community language classes have access to these forms of technology? Unless links can be forged between these and mainstream education, the former will, effectively, be excluded from accessing these resources.

For the Portuguese students, what started as a right to education with a view to returning to Portugal may no longer correspond entirely to their needs. As the community grows and develops, so those needs change. To be properly addressed, they have to be identified and acted upon. The key question is whether the educational, linguistic and cultural characteristics of the children who constitute the Portuguese community now are the same as those of their fellow migrant citizens a generation ago. Clearly, as communities move forward to take up their roles in a Europe where borders are ever more fluid, the needs of bilingual/multilingual children as eurocitizens have to be catered for. This also implies that, if we are to respect individuals within the context of a multifaceted and multicultural society, schools will have to be able to cope with new challenges.

We have reached a point where the 'one model fits all' strategy no longer applies. As European education systems evolve to respond to a changing political and socio-economic reality, we are compelled to reflect on how these systems can include the diversified interests of the communities they serve.

6

Multilingual Learning Stories in Two Gujarati Complementary Schools in Leicester

Peter Martin, Arvind Bhatt, Nirmala Bhojani and Angela Creese

Introduction

In 2002, the publication of a policy paper by the British Home Secretary at the time, David Blunkett, entitled *Integration with Diversity: Globalisation and the Renewal of Democracy and Civil Society* in a volume on *Rethinking Britishness* (Blunkett, 2002) caused a furore in the British press and among some communities in Britain. Following the publication of the paper, *The Times* (16 September 2002), for example, ran the headline 'Immigrants told to speak English even at home'. In the policy paper, Blunkett had made the following statement, to which reference has already been made in the introduction to this volume:

> ... speaking English enables parents to converse with their children in English, as well as their historic mother tongue, at home and to participate in wider modern culture. It helps to overcome the schizophrenia which bedevils generational relationships. In as many as 30% of Asian British households, according to the recent citizenship survey, English is not spoken at home. (Blunkett, 2002:76)

There are several significant issues lurking within this statement which require comment, not least of which is the pejorative use of the term 'schizophrenia' to describe multilingual language practices among the Asian community in Britain. But this statement is all the more odd when put alongside other remarks made by Blunkett in the policy paper. For example, just two paragraphs above this now infamous statement, Blunkett (2002:75-76) stresses that:

> [p]eople must be free to choose how to lead their lives, what religion to follow and so on. Such diversity is not only a right; it is desirable. It brings immense social, economic and cultural benefits to our society.

And he goes on to make reference to the need to 'overcome mutual hostility and ignorance'.

Blunkett's statement tells us much about the way multilingualism is perceived in Britain. Although Edwards (1994:1) emphasises the point that multilingualism is 'a normal and unremarkable necessity for the majority of the world today', the fact that switching between languages, one of the most widespread features of 'multilingualism', can be equated to a psychological illness by a senior British politician is telling indeed.

No less telling is the response of another politician, one from the city of Leicester, the context of this chapter. In the local newspaper, the *Leicester Mercury* (16 September 2002:1), under the headline 'Row: Fury at claim that Asians don't speak enough English in the home', Keith Vaz, the 'prominent Asian MP [Member of Parliament]' for Leicester East, was quoted as saying that 'all Asian families in Leicester do speak English at home'.

In other words, the thrust of the rebuttal to Blunkett's statement was not 'what's wrong with using more than one language in the home?', but rather 'all families speak English at home'. The focus of the response, like the initial statement from Blunkett, suggests what Baetens Beardsmore (2003:10) has referred to as the 'deep-seated and widespread fear of bilingualism'.

The opening discussion above provides a backdrop to our contribution to this volume on multilingual learning stories in schools and communities in Britain. At the outset, we want to emphasise that the wider environment from which these stories emerge is a largely monolingual and 'monolingualising' (Heller, 1995:374) one, despite government rhetoric which purports to endorse and celebrate multilingualism and multiculturalism. Massey (1991:13) has referred to the tokenistic '3S' approach to multicultural education based around 'Saris, Samosas and Steel bands' (Mullard, 1981). Edwards and Redfern (1992:50) have made a similar point about the 'occasional assembly on Diwali or the inclusion of a Caribbean dish in cookery class'. Significantly, although cultural diversity and, to a lesser extent, linguistic diversity, are celebrated and valued, they are usually done so 'without recourse to the social experiences of the speakers of these languages' (Rassool, 1995:288).

This is the background, then, to the story we want to tell in this chapter. We wish to relate some of the multilingual learning experiences in two Gujarati complementary schools in the multilingual city of Leicester in the East Midlands of England, and explore the way that students attending these schools are given the opportunity to reclaim 'the specificity of cultural and social identity that [is] missing from mainstream schooling' (Hall *et al*, 2002: 409). In other words, we wish to focus on how the participants in the school sites manage their multilingualism in the face of the ideologically mono-lingual environment outside the schools.

The chapter emerges from a study carried out in two Leicester comple-mentary schools, between 2003-2004. In the first part there is a brief historical review of migrations into Leicester and the rise of complementary education in the city. In the second part of the chapter, we provide a brief account of the methodology carried out in the initial study. The major discussion in the chapter describes some of the flexible, multilingual learning experiences which we observed, and takes into account the views of the participants in the study.

There are, thus, two main themes which emerge in this study of multilingual learning stories in the two Gujarati complementary schools in Leicester. The first theme is the spontaneity and normality of bilingual conversations in the communities under study. The second theme is the flexibility of such bi-lingual conversations and the way this enables those interacting in the con-versations to contribute to their own multilingual identities.

The Leicester context

Leicester is the largest city in the East Midlands of England, with a population in 2001 of 279,923 (www.leicester.gov.uk). The ethnic minority population is approaching 40% and, given current demographic trends, the city is expected to become the first city in the UK with a non-white ethnic majority popu-lation by 2011. According to Singh (2003:50), Leicester has 'developed a rela-tively successful approach to managing ethnic diversity and promoting tolerance' and has been transformed from the 'most racist' place in the UK in the early 1970s to a 'model of multiculturalism'.

A general account of the histories of migration into England is provided in the volume *The Other Languages of England* (Linguistic Minorities Project, 1985; see also Edwards, 2005; and Ghuman, 2003). In Leicester, it is well docu-mented that over 20,000 East African and Ugandan Asians, who were expelled from Kenya and Uganda, arrived in the city between 1968 and 1973. Singh

(2003) reports that, by the 1991 census, Gujarati East Africans in Leicester comprised about one-fifth of the city's total population. He refers to these groups as 'twice migrants' in that, following a period of settlement in East Africa, they moved on again as a result of the Africanisation policies (Singh, 2003:45).

It has been noted that those migrants who came to Britain via East Africa brought with them a different sociolinguistic profile from those who came directly from the sub-continent (Linguistic Minorities Project, 1985). For example, in East Africa, many of them became fluent in Swahili while others did not become literate in Gujarati due to lack to educational provision at the time of their initial or subsequent migration. A Gujarati saying makes reference to the loss of the three 'Ss' during their migration history: the loss of their culture in the move from India to Africa (*Sanskriti*), the loss of wealth following the expulsion from Africa (*Sampathi*) and, within the UK, the loss of their children as they move away from their familial Indian/African roots and become absorbed by British culture (*Santan*).

Following the large scale migrations into Leicester in the early 1970s, the communities began to organise after hours schools in order to promote their languages and cultures. In fact, the history of such complementary schools in Leicester extends back to the end of the nineteenth century with the opening of the Leicester Hebrew Congregation in 1896.

Given the lack of status accorded to the languages of the new migrants, and the fact that mainstream education in most contexts ignores cultural and linguistic diversity, it is hardly surprising that the communities in Leicester became involved in setting up schools. It is, however, not possible to provide a precise number of complementary schools in Leicester due to the fact that, whereas some schools have a formal constitution and receive a small amount of funding from the Education Department of Leicester City Council, others are less formal and very often convene in private houses.

Leicester City Council acknowledges the important work undertaken by complementary schools in the following areas:

- Teaching heritage languages
- Promoting cultural and faith identity
- Engaging in meaningful learning opportunities
- Providing study support
- Raising educational standards

Leicester City Council
http://www.leicester.gov.uk/your-council—services/education—life
long-learning/about-us/lea-services/multicultural-education/
complementary-schools/partnership-working

Despite the recognition of the value of complementary schools, the Education Authority only provides nominal financial support.

Building on research based at the Universities of Leicester and Birmingham (Martin *et al*, 2003; Martin *et al*, 2004) the Leicester Complementary Schools Trust was established in 2004. This trust not only aims to raise the profile of complementary schooling in the city but, at a pragmatic level, one of the objectives of the Trust is to improve the standards of teaching and learning in complementary schools by devising a training and capacity building programme for staff and students in the schools.

Method

Ethnographic case studies of two Gujarati complementary schools in Leicester were conducted over a period of five months. Both schools were in wards of the city in which a high percentage of the residents belong to an ethnic minority group (Leicestershire County Council, 1991:9-10). Languages spoken in these wards include Gujarati, Panjabi, Urdu and English. School A convenes on one weekday evening a week, from 6 to 8pm in a large, Victorian primary school and community centre building. The number of registered students in School A was 90 at the time of the study. School B meets on Saturday mornings in the premises of a local Community College. The number of students registered in this school at the time of the study was 160.

A variety of methods were used in the study. Over a period of three months, the research team engaged in semi-participant observation in the two schools. This involved ten visits from two members of the research team to each school, on Tuesday evenings and Saturday mornings. These visits included observation of classrooms and assemblies, and a range of other school events. These observations produced detailed field notes on both schools, and documents pertaining to school life were collected. In addition, four lessons were audio-recorded, with the full permission of the head teachers and all participants.

As well as the observations, two types of semi-structured interviews were used. Four separate, though overlapping, interview schedules were used to interview administrators, teachers, parents, and students. Individual interviews were held with the senior administrators or head teachers in each school, and two teachers in each school. In addition, interviews were held with two parents and one individual student. Group interviews were held with three groups of students. All interviews were audio-recorded with the permission of the school administrator or head teacher and the interviewees, and transcribed and translated into English where necessary.

The theoretical and methodological framework for the analysis of the data draws on anthropological linguistics, including interactional sociolinguistics (Gumperz, 1982) and the Ethnography of Communication (Hymes, 1974). This framework was used to look at teacher/student interactions, code-switching, and the discursive construction by complementary school participants of identity, language, literacy and learning. Within this framework, observational field notes were analysed and written up as vignettes to illustrate emerging patterns.

Multilingualism in use

In this section of the chapter we report mainly on what we observed and recorded in the classrooms and on the interviews with participants in the study. A full report of the study is available in Martin *et al* (2004). In work published elsewhere, we have focused on particular aspects emerging from the study: links between complementary and mainstream schools (Bhatt *et al*, 2004), multicultural, heritage and learner identities in the schools (Creese *et al*, 2006), and bilingual interaction in the schools (Martin *et al*, 2006).

In this chapter, we focus on what we have called the flexible, multilingual nature of talk in the schools and, at the same time, we explore the views of the participants in the study about their use of two languages. In so doing, in line with the themes of the volume, we aim to relate our story about multilingualism in use in the two school environments. We first provide some initial thoughts, based largely on the final report of the initial study (Martin *et al*, 2004) in order to provide a summary of the way Gujarati and English are used together in the classroom.

In both schools, in the classrooms, there is detailed careful work around learning of the Gujarati script, the formation of letters, as well as on pronunciation. Much of the discussion around this learning is in English, although the amount of English used depends on the particular class teacher and on the level of the class. English is noticeably the language of clarification and explanation, and the language used by students in asking questions.

The classroom participants use a range of bilingual strategies similar to those reported in other multilingual classroom environments (Arthur and Martin,

2006). A common strategy, for example, is embedding a Gujarati word into a question in English. For example, while writing the date on the chalkboard the teacher asks 'What does *tarikh* mean?', and students respond 'date'. A similar strategy occurs in other classrooms, but in Gujarati, for example, '*bari etle*?' ('window what means?'), to which a student responds 'window'. These sorts of bilingual 'label quests' (Heath, 1986) are common in the classroom, and resonate with strategies used in other bilingual contexts.

Negotiation of meaning usually takes place in English, as in the exchange where the teacher asks 'do you know what *chanchal* means?' and when there is no response she says 'the person who does not sit still'. A student then offers 'fidgeting' to which the teacher responds 'yes, fidgeting, but in a nice way'.

An interesting contrast occurs between the two schools and, in particular, how the two head teachers use language in assemblies and around the school. In School A, the head teacher uses a type of upbeat modern youth discourse in English, and switches into Gujarati to make reference to specific cultural events and activities. In School B, on the other hand, the head teacher uses Gujarati more frequently, and when she switches to English, for example to repeat specific instructions or for disciplinary measures, it is a more formal type of English than the head teacher's in School A.

Perhaps the most significant issue in our discussion of classroom discourses in the two schools is the way that bilingualism and bilingual teaching and learning are managed. Bilingualism is not part of the mainstream educational agenda, but in complementary schools we find two languages occurring side by side in an unproblematic and uncontested way. Although, on occasions in the classrooms, some teachers urged the students to 'speak Gujarati', the most noticeable feature of the discourses of the two schools and their classrooms is the skilful and spontaneous juxtaposition of English and Gujarati.

The discussion above demonstrates the bilingual strategies used by the teachers and students in the schools in this study. Of particular note is the way the two languages, Gujarati and English, come together in order to accomplish teaching and learning and, we would suggest, to underscore the fluid identities of the participants in the lessons. With regard to the use of both Gujarati and English, both the head teachers make comments which suggest that they are at ease with switching between languages. For example, the head teacher in School A, when asked which language she wanted to be interviewed in, responded:

I prefer both languages. *Because I am happy with both languages ... ask me in English* ... then I can choose which language to answer in. [italics – in Gujarati] (Head teacher, School A)

In response to a question about the use of two languages, the head teacher in School B responded:

Two heads is better than one... so two languages is always better than one and it gives them extra self confidence thinking I am not monolingual ... I'm bilingual. We're teaching the value of the mother tongue as well as the behaviour, discipline that goes with it. (Head teacher, School B)

Neither of these two teachers problematises the use of both English and Gujarati together and they do not seem to be affected by ideologies which exist in the wider, 'monolingualising' environment. One of the teachers in School A, who is also a head teacher in another large Gujarati school, similarly explains:

So we try to explain in English ... because at the end we ask them what a Gujarati word means in English... because that's how they should be thinking at the same time .. so sometimes you have to use English to make them understand. (Teacher, School A)

The students, too, often make reference to switching between Gujarati and English in the home. In a group interview, the following statements made by two students all show that switching between languages, far from being 'schizophrenic', is a normal part of a bilingual's language behaviour.

I speak English and Gujarati mixed. I don't stick to one language. Sometimes I get told off by my Mum.

Sometimes my dad likes to speak Gujarati so I speak it for like five minutes then I'm back to English, but sometimes it's mixed. (Group interview with students in School B)

Further examples of 'multilingualism in use' are provided by the head teachers during assemblies. For example, our field notes provide the following description of language use in one assembly in School A:

Deepa blows the whistle to signal the start of the assembly. Students line up with teachers and assistants standing in front. Deepa takes the lead in reminding students about the *holi* festival (on Monday 17th March) and *dhuleti* which is today. There is a hum and chatter while she speaks. She walks to the group of students who seem to be noisier. She starts in Gujarati asking how do we celebrate *holi*? Switches to English to explain the use of popcorn made from *juwar* (Gujarati corn). Continues in English to ask why do we throw colours. (Fieldnotes, Assembly, School A, 18.03.2003)

In this particular assembly, the head teacher is using both languages. She emphasises aspects of discipline in English and often switches to Gujarati to talk about cultural events. At the beginning of the assembly Deepa has asked the children 'what is special about today?'. Incidentally, the response of one child that it is St Patrick's Day causes some mirth and Deepa responded that St Patrick's Day 'was yesterday'. This incident, though, does demonstrate the complex cultural world in which the students live.

In School, B, the head teacher also uses two languages in the assembly which, as in the other school, is not only a cultural event but also a channel to provide information to the students and to those parents who attend. In one assembly, held the day before the cricket world cup final in which India were due to play Australia, there was a lot of talk about the match, in both Gujarati and English. There was also talk about the war in Iraq:

> She says that there will be special prayers today. She asks them why, and one student replies 'We want India to win'. She asks if there is any other reason, and another child says 'We want the war to end'. She asks them what 'war' is called in Gujarati and gets two answers, both correct. (Fieldnotes, Assembly, School A, 22.03.2003)

We now turn to what is actually going on in the classrooms. An excerpt from our fieldnotes provides an account of how two languages are used in one particular class, in which the teacher is represented by SB:

> As I enter the class, the students are revising the Indian national anthem. There are four boys and nine girls. The class sings the anthem. SB reminds them to 'learn it properly' in English as it is written in their books in Gujarati. SB uses Gujarati but peppers it with English for emphasis or ease of communication. The students are quiet and attentive. They have their exercise books and a sheet of printed Gujarati prayer in front of them. She goes on to revise tenses. She does this standing up and talking in Gujarati. She goes through a list of questions that could be asked in an exam. She tells them how the questions could be answered: '*sawal poocchhe* to answer the question'. She upbraids some students who are apparently not paying enough attention: *tran-char jan haji* think *kare chhe. Haji* answer *aapwano chhe*'. When SB asks students to answer, they reply in English. SB accepts that as indication that they have understood. She says things like: *aapne bolie* to sound *baraber thay chhe; swad etle shu*? (student answers: taste). SB tells them that they may be required to match food items to different tastes. She then goes over other topics for exams: directions, professions, gender inflections. SB revises these with examples. Some girls are taking notes as SB speaks but most listen or speak. SB practices: *soorya poorva dishama oogey chhe* ('sun rises in the east'). She writes the words for sun and east on the whiteboard. She has already written the date and the day

and *jai jalaram* in Gujarati on the whiteboard. She has a small portrait of Jalaram propped up against her bag on the table. She revises masculine and feminine: king-queen, father-mother, male and female teacher and, interestingly, washerman (*dhobi*) and washerwoman (*dhoban*). She then revises singular and plural and shows students a printed sheet in Gujarati to indicate what is expected of them. She reminds students about the possibility of translation in the exam: words*nu* translation *aawshe*, sentence*nu* translation *aawshe*, holidays *pahela be swadhyay aapya hata*. She then checks orally the homework given during the holidays. Students mark their own work. (Fieldnotes, School B, 07.06.2003)

This set of fieldnotes shows how languages and literacies are used in a range of ways. Switches in language use occur between teacher and student, and also within teacher utterances (between statements, within statements and even within lexemes). Some actual examples of the discourse of two classrooms will be provided below, but this excerpt from our fieldnotes demonstrates clearly the multilingual nature of language use in the class.

The extracts below come from two classrooms, both in School A. It is not the purpose here to describe the pedagogical processes at work in the classroom, but rather to tell the story of how two teachers and two groups of students rely on two languages in order to accomplish the lesson. The first extract comes from a class of 22 students, ranging from 7-11 years of age. The teacher, whom we have called Mrs Solanki, had been teaching Gujarati in England for sixteen years at the time of the study.

Extract 1 below comes from near the end of a lesson. The teacher and students have been negotiating an end of class activity and this is done mainly in English.

Transcription conventions

T	Teacher
S	Student
Bold font	**Gujarati**
Italics	*<English gloss>*

Extract 1:

S: you give us the English word and we give you the Gujarati word.
    please Miss . please

T: I was going to do a story but we haven't the time for it

S: you give us the English. we give you the Gujarati

T: right . listen . we do the story next week . [chatter] . right . **sambhlo badha**

<listen everyone> . stop making a fuss . you have to see what I am doing and I will tell you what to do as well and reply in Gujarati in full sentences

S: then you can see the English meaning in Gujarati

T: **maro . sambhal** *<my . listen>* . I will choose anybody . **maro hath kya chhe?** *<where is my hand?>* . don't forget . yeah? **Maro hath kya chhe?**

S: **tamaro hath . ooper chhe** *<your hand is on>*

T: right . good

S: **tamaro hath . kapal** *<your hand . forehead>*

T: **tamaro hath tamara kapal ooper chhe** *<your hand is on your forehead>* sorry? **ooper chhe** *<is on>* . right . how can it be a proper sentence . Neil?

S: **tamaro hath tamara kapal ooper chhe** *<your hand is on your forehead>*

T: good . OK . it should be **tamaro hath tamara kapal ooper chhe . tamari ankhno rung kewo chhe? Tamari ankhno rung kewo chhe?** *<what colour are your eyes?>*

S: **tamari** *<your>*

T: just a minute . **tamari ankhno rung kewo chhe?** *<what colour are your eyes?* Dixita . **tamari ankhno rung kewo chhe?** . *<what colour are your eyes?>* don't want the answer in English . yeah you can say . come on . you can say it . how to say it? Do you understand the question? **Tamari ankhno rung kewo chhe?** *<what colour are your eyes?>* First of all . you gotta say 'my' . so how would you say that? . **mari** *<my>* OK? And then the next bit is . **mari ankhno** *<of my eyes>* and then? . **rung** *<colour>* . and the word for black? . **kalo . chhe** . *<is black>* right . the whole sentence together now

S: **mari ankhno rung kalo chhe** *<the colour of my eye is black>*

T: well done . **mari ankhno rung kalo chhe** *<the colour of my eyes is black>* . **bey ankh wachey** *<between the two eyes>* Jaina . concentrate . **shu aawelu chhe?** *(what is between?)* don't forget . I want the answer in full sentence . right? **Shu aawelu chhe?** *<what is?>*

S: **bey ankhni wachey naak chhe** *<the nose is between the eyes>*

T: OK . very good

As can be seen from the start of Extract 1, the students are hoping for an activity which involves both languages, that is, where they provide Gujarati words for words given in English. This is an activity which they have enjoyed in previous lessons, and one with which they are familiar. However, the teacher decides on a game in which she mimes a simple action and the students are required to 'reply in Gujarati in full sentences'. As will be clear from the extract, this activity is actually a type of drilling game in which the students follow the structure provided by the teacher.

The statements at the beginning of Extract 1 are quite telling in that they illustrate the significance of both English and Gujarati in the learning process (Bhatt *et al*, 2004), and they also show how translation, despite being an unfashionable skill in language learning, is part of the usual discourse of this classroom and, indeed, in others that we observed. Towards the end of this abstract, the discourse moves away from pure translation to a type of discourse where the students are building on their knowledge of Gujarati and the structures introduced earlier in the discourse, in order to construct quite complex sentences.

In this extract then, there are elements of drilling and translation, both of which might be considered to come from an earlier era of language teaching. But we would contend that in using both languages in the conversation, through the use of a typical Initiation-Response-Evaluation/Feedback exchange structure, the teachers and learners are inculcating use of the language in meaningful ways.

The next three extracts all come from one lesson in a class of 11-14 year olds who are taking their GCSE (General Certificate of Secondary Education) in Gujarati. The teacher is Mr Patel, who had previously taught Gujarati in government schools in Kenya from 1974 to 1982, and has been teaching Gujarati in England since 1989, in several schools, including as headteacher and administrator in a complementary school.

The context of the first extract from this class (Extract Two, below) is that the teacher and students are going through a letter written in Gujarati. It will be noted immediately that, in this extract, more Gujarati is used and this is to be expected, given that these students are at a higher level and are shortly to be taking GCSE Gujarati. Although there is more Gujarati spoken in this extract, it is noticeable that most of the student responses are in English.

Extract 2:

T: very good . OK . ***kem chhe*** . *<how are you>* **etle kyare pun apne** letter writing **kariye to** formal . *<it means when we do* letter writing *we have to write* formal> **kem chho . ahi badhani tabiyat barabar chhe . etle shun**? *<how are you . everybody is well here . what does that mean?>*

S: [attempts to answer]

114

T: **badha .. ena pachhi je wakya chhe te . natakma bhag lidho hato tena wishe wanchine anand thayo .. etle shu**? <*all .. now the next sentence . was happy to read about (you) taking part in a play .. what does that mean?*>

S: took part in a play

T: play . **natak etle**? <*what does play mean?*>

S: play

T: play . **bijo kayo shabda hashey** <*what is another word for play?*>

S: drama

T: drama . **dramama bhag lidho hato** . <*took part in a drama*> **Yusufne kagal lakhey chhe . kon kagal lakhey chhe aa? Yusufne kon kagal lakhey chhe . Aakash?** <*writing a letter to Yusuf . who's writing it? Who is writing to Yusuf?*> **. Aakash?**

S: ... Kamal

T: Kamal . **saras** <*good*> . good . excellent . **Kamal Yusufne kagal lakhey chhe** <*Kamal is writing to Yusuf*> . OK . Tushar **bijo** <*second*> paragraph

Particularly interesting, perhaps, is the way the teacher and students unpack the meaning of the term **natak** ('play'). In the teacher's second utterance he is reading and annotating the letter, and he asks the students, in Gujarati, what the sentence means. One student provides a translation ('took part in a play') and then the teacher proceeds to check that the students are familiar with the word in both languages.

Later in the same lesson the teacher and students are talking about wedding ceremonies. In Extract 3 below, it can be noted that there is a lot of cultural content in the discussion, and there is no pressure on the part of the students to use Gujarati. The lack of any pressure from the teacher allows for more spontaneous discussion and for cultural issues to come to the fore.

Extract 3:

T: **biju ek wastu . tya lagna widhi thati hoi** . OK . **tame** bore **thata hoi to** wedding ceremony **jowanama** bore **thatu hoi tamne?** <*one more thing . the wedding ceremony there . OK . do you get bored looking at the ceremony?*>

S: **ha** <*yes*>

T: **kem?** <*why?*>

S: [indistinct]

T: that's the main objective . **lagna prsang etle** <*marriage*> . wedding ceremony

S: I've seen it twice

T: **bey wakhat joyu chhe? Te pun joyu chhe?** <*you've seen it twice? You as well?*> . OK . **to have ema bijo** point **ave ke e widhi** ceremony **tamne lambi lago ohho?** <OK . the second point is do you feel that the ceremony is long> long ceremony or .

S: [Many ss speak at once]

T: cut it to one hour from three hours . supposing you getting married . you want to get married in a three-hour long ceremony?

S: no . an hour

T: [indistinct English] **bau widhi lambi hoi . trun char kalakni** <*very long ceremony . three or four hours*> . takes four hours and you get bored . so what thing . how can things change?

S: cut down the photographs

T: cut down the photographs? Yeah . you are right there . [laughter] . because all you see are the photographers . videos and people . all surrounding the bride and groom

S: you can hardly see anything

T: so you can't see anything

S: [indistinct English]

T: so . yes . that's a good reason . yes . **ghana lagnama** photographer **ane** video **ootarta hoi . e loko akho mandap** cover up **kari le . barabar . ne** ceremony**ma shu thai chhe** <*during many weddings there are* photographers *and* videos *are taken . these people* cover *all the wedding stage right? You don't know what is happening in the* ceremony> . good reason . OK . that's OK . so do you like to go or not?

S: [respond in English, indistinct]

T: at least you got some positive answer . OK . **have tane jawu gamey ke nai?** <*you like going?*> **saras** . <*good*> OK

The students appear keen to take part in the discussion, as wedding ceremonies are something they have all attended. The cultural content of the lesson is a very important aim of the school. The teacher, Mr Patel, in an interview notes that:

> You can't separate language and culture ... how the different festivals are celebrated are all part of the culture. (Interview with Mr Patel, School A)

The final extract from the GCSE class comes towards the end of the lesson when Mr Patel is setting homework for the class. There is no interaction in this extract. Rather it is a teacher monologue which consists of mixed Gujarati and English discourse, consisting of switches between utterances, within utterances and even at the word level. The topic for homework is 'different types of wedding ceremony in different religions', a topic closely linked to culture.

Extract 4:

T: OK . that's good . that's good news from everybody . **have** <*now*> your next homework would be . speaking . different religions have different ways of . wedding ceremonies . Islam **lokoni** different **widhi hoi** . <*Islam has different ways*> Christian **lokoni judi hoi** <*Christians have different ways*> . **pachhi** Buddhism **e lokoni judi hoi** <*then Buddhism has different ways*> . **Hinduismni judi hoi** <*Hinduism has different ways*> . **to tamare** next week **jyare tame aawo . aawta** week**thi** <*so you . when you come* next week . *in the coming week*> . I would like to get some information on wedding ceremonies . it is very important because we must learn all the cultures . that's very important . **badhi Sanskrit hoi badha dharamni** <*you must be aware of all the cultures*> . we must . it's very important . that we learn to be good citizen . that's how it should be . **to** <*so the*> homework **aawta atthwadia mate** <*for next week is*> wedding ceremonies **ma** <*in*> different religions . **teo kewi ritey** <*how do they*> . **bolwaan chhe** <*only have to speak*> . **tame lakhi shako chho** <*you can write*> . you can write it **pun bolwa mate** <*but for speaking*> . speaking . for speaking purpose . OK? **Tame mandire jau** <*you can go to the temple*> . temple . church**ma jau** <*to a church*> . **masjidma jau** <*to a mosque*> . mosque . **tamara** friends . <*you may have* friends> **hoi . koi Muslim mitra hoi to ene poochhwanu** . <*if you have a* Muslim *friend you ask them*> . try to get information on the different religions . how the wedding ceremony . OK

As noted above, Mr Patel's speech is a mixture of English and Gujarati, with key points and terms in both languages. What we suggest is happening here is that the teacher is skilfully and spontaneously synthesising his linguistic resources in a natural way in order to promote bilingual and bicultural learning.

In the extracts from Mr Patel's class, it is clear how cultural references are woven into the fabric of the lesson. Two languages are used to do this. Even though in Extract Three much of the conversation is in English, the conversation develops a strong cultural consonance between teacher and learners and contributes to the identity construction that underpins the lesson. This is reiterated in Extract Four, in which Mr Patel stresses that knowing about different cultures is important in order to be a good citizen. This brings us back to the discussion at the beginning of the paper, showing how the multilingual learning stories in these schools offer a different model of citizenship from that suggested in Blunkett's remarks and from the '3S' approach to multicultural education. The stories told here suggest a more hands-on, genuine type of multicultural and multilingual education, embedded in the learners' real life experiences.

Conclusions

In this chapter we set out to describe some of the multilingual learning experiences in two Gujarati schools in Leicester. The interview data, and observational fieldnotes and the classroom extracts tell a story of how people involved in the study bring together their 'different worlds' (Kenner, 2004a) through the bilingual discourse. This use of two languages, according to the participants in the study, also occurs in the home. But the fact that such discourse is also part of their schooling goes beyond the celebration of language to a spontaneous educational experience which is inclusive and empowering and, at the same time, challenges the monolingualising ideologies in the wider environment. Critically, the use of Gujarati alongside English affirms the importance of Gujarati in relation to different types of identities, including multicultural, heritage and learner identities (Creese *et al*, 2006; Hall *et al*, 2002).

As Hall *et al* (2002: 415) note, although complementary schools might contain 'elements of cultural resistance', they play a major part in 'filling in the gaps of cultural specificity that mainstream schooling neglects'. The message we thus wish to put forward in this chapter is how these schools fill in the gaps and demonstrate the normality of multilingualism.

We wish to acknowledge the support of the ESRC (R000223949).

7

Culture, Languages and Learning: mediating a bilingual approach in complementary Saturday classes

Jean Conteh

Introduction

In this chapter, I describe the work of the teachers in some complementary classes which have been operating in the city of Bradford since 2003. They were initiated by three young, newly qualified bilingual primary teachers who wanted to use their skills to help to improve the lives of members of their own communities. The classes are unusual in that they do not aim to teach children to read and write their mother tongues, nor do they have the long-term intentions of helping pupils sit GCSEs or A-levels. Instead, they aim to develop emergent bilingual children's knowledge of and confidence in their home and community languages as a means of raising their achievements in mainstream schooling. In so doing, they contribute to maintaining heritage languages in the community.

The teachers have constructed what can be described as a bilingual approach to teaching and learning. They promote the children's ability to use their home languages as a tool for learning the concepts and knowledge of the National Curriculum. They actively encourage the children to make links between the work they do in the Saturday classes and in their mainstream classrooms and so help to raise their achievements in their mainstream learning.

I focus on the work of the teachers, contextualising it in national policies related to language in primary schools in England and in theories of bilingualism, culture and learning. In this way, I raise questions about how the professional roles and identities of bilingual teachers are currently constructed in mainstream contexts. Some examples of classroom interaction from the classes are provided to show how the teachers work with their pupils, demonstrating how their practices are grounded in their own experiences as learners and in their professional knowledge. I conclude with some brief insights into the children's and their parents' views and opinions about the classes.

Background: language, cultural awareness and a bilingual approach

On a chilly Saturday morning in March, about 40 adults and children gathered in a classroom in a small primary school in inner city Bradford. Some of the adults were international students, from Brunei, Taiwan and China. They were pursuing MA courses in education at a university in the region and had been invited to the classes to see how the teachers were developing what they called a bilingual approach to learning in their work with the children.

The teachers who run the Saturday classes are qualified primary teachers who work in other schools in the city through the week. Most of the group of 40 were children who had turned up for their regular bilingual Saturday classes, as they had been doing since the previous September. They attend the school, or others nearby, through the week.

The school was named after the imposing Victorian textile mill which towers over the houses in which many of the children's families live. The mill at one time provided employment for most of the local community, including the families originally from Pakistan and Bangladesh who settled in the area in the years after the Second World War. Now, it was in the process of being converted into penthouse and studio apartments for young urban professionals and was attracting many buyers from all over the country. The children and grandchildren of the millworkers from the Indian subcontinent were those now attending schools in the area.

The range of languages represented in the classroom on this particular morning was wide – the ones usually present, spoken by the children and their teachers: English, Punjabi, Hinko, Urdu and Bangla, were added to by Mandarin, Taiwanese, Malay, Gujerati and probably one or two others. What resulted from this meeting of such a diverse group of individuals was a lively two-hour session containing a wealth of activities, all focusing on language awareness and learning about language, carried out in a rich context of cultural diversity.

Among other things, we learned to count in Chinese, Malay and Urdu, and how to write our names in the three different scripts. We compared the same sentences written in Urdu and Arabic scripts. We listened to an Urdu *naath*, a poem composed according to a tightly defined syllabic scheme, rhythmically declaimed by a 9-year old girl, Humah. Her Urdu literacy – learnt at home from her mother – was of a high level. We also gained a few nuggets of cultural knowledge; why, for example, blocks of flats in Taiwan never have a 4th floor and why it is rude in Brunei to call someone 'you'.

It was difficult to tell who were the teachers and who the learners. Children and adults shared teaching and learning roles, each developing language and cultural awareness and making links between their own experiences and new knowledge in fascinating and complex ways. Such links are part of what Cummins (2001:2) describes as 'negotiating identities' and argues are 'fundamental to the academic success of culturally diverse students' – indeed, all students.

One memorable moment happened when one of the MA students, Ali, from Brunei, wrote the full name of his country (*Negara Brunei Darussalam*) on the whiteboard in Arabic script and explained to the children that it meant 'State of Brunei, abode of peace'. One of the adults listening, Ibrahim, who was born in Malawi into a Gujerati-speaking family and moved to England at the age of 14, was amazed to hear the name and immediately linked it with his childhood memories of Swahili and of East African placenames.

Humah, the *naath* reciter, spotted links with her own language knowledge, and went up to the whiteboard to write the name in Urdu script beneath Ali's Arabic version. She was then able to analyse the similarities and differences between the two scripts, pointing different features out to Ali and the rest of us. Both Ibrahim and Humah were able to use the knowledge they brought to the classroom to learn something new, and both were subsequently able to teach the rest of us something. In the process, their confidence grew – Humah's almost visibly – as did their self-identity as learners.

Some brief quotes from the children's thank you letters to the students capture the pleasure they gained from the morning, as well as their self-confidence in their own knowledge and the dialogic nature of their learning:

> ... I enjoyed learning your language with us ..... I hope you enjoyed listening to my *naath* when I was singing ... (Humah, aged 9)

... thank you for coming and visiting us and sharing your stories, numbers and your language. We hope you enjoyed visiting us, learning our numbers in Urdu and Punjabi .... I also enjoyed listening to the fourth floor story (not)... (Irfan, aged 8)

... My favourite activity was when we looked at the map and I liked the country called Brunei. I liked it when we talked in Punjabi. I liked it when we spoke in Chinese and Taiwanese. Ali's language was fun to learn ... (Haineh, aged 8)

Like many other complementary classes in Britain, the one described in this chapter takes place in a mainstream school building, when the school's normal business is over for the week. Unlike many classes, however, one of the explicit intentions is to make links between complementary and mainstream learning. The teachers, who are all qualified primary teachers, intentionally use as far as possible the same approaches and strategies in both contexts, sometimes mediating the same learning objectives. In doing so, they aim to support the children's learning in mainstream classes and improve their access to the National Curriculum, particularly English and Maths. The hope is that this will develop the children's self-confidence as learners and help raise their achievements in the Key Stage Two SATs – the tests completed by all 11-year olds at the end of their primary education – and other national assessments.

But there is one big difference in the teachers' practices between mainstream and complementary contexts. In the Saturday classes, both teachers and pupils are bilingual, indeed – in many cases – multilingual. Qualified bilingual teachers are still very much in the minority in mainstream contexts in England, and the possible advantages of their bilingualism for their professional roles are virtually unrecognised.

In the Saturday classes, however, the teachers facilitate the use of a range of languages in the processes of teaching and learning. Their key aim in doing this is to open out the full potential for the children's learning by allowing them to use their knowledge of all the languages they have at their disposal. In this, they are applying Cummins' (2001:104ff) 'additive bilingualism enrichment' principles and challenging some of the naturalised and intuitively seductive notions which many teachers hold about how children learn additional languages. Equally importantly, they are also developing their own skills and strategies, and their professional identities as bilingual teachers, something in which they can feel quite constrained in mainstream school.

This focus on bilingual learning is, of course, supported by the fact that they share the same languages as some of their pupils. But this does not prevent the teachers from allowing the children to use their own languages, when they are different. A small but significant number of children attending the classes speak other languages than the Urdu, Punjabi and Bangla spoken by their teachers, who see these languages as part of the valuable 'funds of knowledge' (Moll *et al*, 1992) which the children bring to their learning. They invite the children to share their language knowledge with their classmates in games and problem-solving activities. They encourage parents to take part in activities and to share what knowledge they have of different languages and scripts.

As the visit from the international students shows, the children are exposed to new languages as much as possible. They are encouraged actively to compare the ways in which meanings are expressed in different languages. The visitors were able to develop the children's awareness of other languages, of the similarities and differences between those languages and their own, and more generally of ways in which thoughts and ideas can be transferred between and across languages.

This is all great fun, of course. But it is more than just a pleasant social activity; it is a vital aspect of cognitive learning and development. As such, it has clear links with the Government's *Excellence and Enjoyment* strategy (DfES, 2003b), for example, with the principles of good learning and teaching (p29) and the anticipated outcomes of promoting creativity (p31).

Supporting bilingualism and cultures of learning: policy and theory

What the teachers are doing in the Saturday classes connects with other recent national policies related to language in primary schools in Britain, and two will briefly be discussed here. In 2003, the DfES funded a pilot study into provision for 'advanced' EAL learners at Key Stage 2 (National Association for Language Development in the Curriculum, 2004). The EAL Pilot Project, as it came to be known, was the first officially funded partnership between the Primary National Strategy and the Ethnic Minority Achievement Project teams in the DfES.

This in itself made it a remarkable initiative. It operated in 21 LEAs, including Bradford, most of which catered for large ethnic minority populations. The project document makes clear how its principles relate to the National Curriculum 2000 statement on inclusion (National Association for Language Development in the Curriculum, 2004:2). It also openly recognises the importance of promoting additive bilingualism. It makes explicit in two of its key principles the potentially positive outcomes for children's learning of supporting and promoting bilingualism in mainstream school:

■ Bilingualism is a valuable asset and first language has a continuing and significant role in learning

■ Language acquisition goes hand in hand with cognitive and academic development (NALDIC, 2004:2)

Thus the work, in its original conception, was theoretically grounded in research into the educational achievements of bilingual learners, though perhaps it did not make the importance of links between bilingualism and identity (Conteh, 2006b:3) as clear as they might be. Since the completion of the pilot, which has had variable success in different parts of the country, longer-term programmes have been developed. For example, in Bradford the links between the EMA and EAL teams continue to be strengthened as the two teams continue to work together. This collaboration has led to the development of approaches for promoting talk for learning and using pupils' whole language repertoires, and a bank of classroom strategies and resources called *Talk across the Curriculum* (Education Bradford, 2006).

The second initiative, the *Languages for All: Languages for Life* strategy, has perhaps greater potential for promoting the kind of language awareness and identity work which the teachers do in the Saturday classes. It was introduced in 2002 (DfES, 2002b) and laid down long-term objectives aimed, among other things, towards introducing modern foreign languages at Key Stage Two into all primary schools by 2010. In the 2002 document, there is a recognition of the potential links between 'modern foreign' languages and 'community' languages.

This could offer important and exciting prospects for bilingual teachers, such as those who run the Saturday classes, in introducing their pupils to new languages, promoting language awareness and, in the process, raising their awareness of the languages which are part of their community knowledge. There is also some awareness of the notion that, if their language repertoires are positively recognised, bilingual children – such as those who attend the Saturday classes – could be at an advantage compared to monolingual pupils in their learning of French, German or Spanish in school.

But the second document connected with this initiative, the *Key Stage 2 Framework for Languages* (DfES, 2005a) is not so clear about this. And, worryingly, this is the statutory document, the one which prescribes what should actually happen in classrooms. It offers no real opportunities for teachers to use or develop links between the different languages that their pupils may bring to their classrooms as a means of supporting their learning of new languages, or to see any languages which they themselves speak as resources for their teaching. There are no suggestions for ways of developing genuinely bilingual teaching approaches, or of helping children use the languages which they bring from home as positive starting-points for their learning of new languages. Indeed, the opposite view can be inferred. At several points, concern is expressed that 'children for whom English is a second or additional language' may need to overcome 'potential barriers to learning' (Part Two:11) and need extra support. And so, they are cast once again into the deficit role.

As we suggested in the introduction, making links between culture, language and identity is crucial for successful learning to take place and for pupils' self-confidence to grow. It is also very important for teaching. The *Framework for Languages* seems to have a confused understanding of these links. Three strands of activity are recommended for each year of Key Stage Two: these are *Oracy, Literacy* and *Intercultural Understanding*. The oracy and literacy activities, in general, are simplified versions of the kinds of activities regularly recommended in MFL materials for secondary pupils. They provide interesting opportunities for extensive repetition and reinforcement of the target language, but not much opportunity for linking with prior knowledge or keying into the 'funds of knowledge' of the community in which the school is based. In the *Intercultural Understanding* strand 'cultural activities' are recommended, such as:

- Compile a list of languages spoken within the school. (Year 3:29)

- Listen to authentic songs linked to celebrations and learn a few key phrases. (Year 4:41)

- Follow a simple recipe and prepare a dish. (Year 5:53)

- Create a multi-media presentation using simple sentences to present information about another culture. (Year 6:64)

Activities such as these almost seem to be a depressing throwback to the 'samosas, saris and steel bands' approach to cultural diversity of the 1970s in the way they represent a fixed and static model of culture and cultural interchange. They fail to recognise the fluid, shifting nature of culture, which is the experience of most of us as we mediate our relationships with others in our daily lives. As Nieto (1999) argues, the dialectical, often contradictory, attributes of culture are played out in all the activities in which we participate and these aspects of students' identities need to be recognised.

The complex intertwining of culture and identity in learning need to be much more fully understood by policy makers. Learning is much more than a set of psychological cognitive processes. Cultural psychologists such as Cole (1996: 131ff) make a strong case for a model of learning as 'situated cognition', nested within concentric layers of context formed by the interactions between teachers and pupils, the specific classroom where these interactions take place, the school, the community, the wider society and so on. He reminds us of the co-constructive nature of these interactions. Both teachers and learners are active participants, forming relationships which, to a greater or lesser extent, afford them spaces to negotiate their personal and cultural identities. Cummins (2001) introduces a clear political element into this model of teaching and learning, arguing that, if issues of cultural and language diversity can be incorporated into the processes of teaching and learning (p137), such negotiations have transformative power:

> When powerful relationships are established between teachers and students, these relationships frequently can transcend the economic and social disadvantages that afflict communities and schools alike in inner city and rural areas. (pp1-2)

As we argued in the introduction, our understanding of the role of culture in teaching and learning is enhanced by the many classic ethnographic texts which reveal the dissonances between home and school for children from different backgrounds to their teachers (see references in the introduction, p17). The knowledge gained from such research is also invaluable in understanding issues of achievement. Studies such as these cumulatively develop a model of 'culturally relevant pedagogy' (Osborne, 1996), which resonates closely with much of what the teachers do in the Saturday classes.

Osborne (p285) provides a list of 'nine assertions' necessary for constructing culturally relevant pedagogy which, he claims, offer us both a 'theoretical perspective' and 'a series of informed and tentative starting points' for developing classroom practice. It is useful to reproduce the assertions here, as a frame for considering the teachers' practices, which are described in the next section. The list is slightly re-ordered, beginning with the assertions which most closely relate to wider contexts and moving progressively inwards, in order to reflect the approach to thinking about learning as situated cognition, nested within concentric layers of context:

- ■ Racism is institutionalised in schools, as in other spaces where members of different ethnic groups come together. This needs addressing, and it can be, in appropriate ways.

- ■ Socio-historico-political realities beyond the school constrain much of what happens in classrooms and must be understood by the culturally relevant teacher.

■ It is important to involve parents and families in their children's learning.

■ Culturally relevant teachers need not come from the same ethnic minority group as the students they teach.

■ Culturally relevant teachers are personally warm toward and respectful of, as well as academically demanding of, all their students.

■ Teachers who teach in culturally relevant ways spell out the cultural assumptions on which the class and the school operate.

■ There are five components of culturally relevant classroom management: using group work, avoiding confrontation, avoiding spotlighting individual children, using an unhurried pace, using the home participation structures of the children, especially in the early stages.

■ It is desirable to include students' first languages in classroom interactions and in the wider school context.

■ It is important to teach content that is culturally relevant to students' previous experiences, that fosters their cultural identity and empowers them with knowledge and practices to operate successfully in mainstream society.

The teachers' views: roles, identities and classroom strategies

The three teachers who run the Saturday classes are all members of local South Asian-heritage communities who have been settled in Bradford (as in similar cities elsewhere in Britain) for two or three generations (Conteh, 2003). They have all been pupils in the education system in which they currently work as teachers. As such, they are part of a small, but growing, group of qualified ethnic minority teachers who are seen, in official discourses, as having a vital role to play in raising the achievements of pupils from different language and cultural backgrounds. Ross (2002:2) articulates the nature of this role, and warns of the dangers if it is not allowed to develop to its fullest potential:

> With such a range of teachers, we can aspire towards delivering an education that has the subtlety and the nuance to make each individual feel that her or his cultural set is acknowledged and valued, thus empowering her or him as a learner. Without such a range of teachers, this cannot even be an aspiration.

Through their personal – and sometimes painful – experiences of the education system as both pupils and teachers, ethnic minority teachers often have a deep knowledge of the issues that pupils currently face, and sophisticated skills in mediating diverse learning settings. At the same time, they are often acutely aware that their professional identities – of which language and bilingualism are important elements – can be called into question by the wider system within which they are working. It is probably true to say that they have all, from time to time, experienced the naturalised, institutional racism which is part of the daily life of most schools.

All three teachers in the classes, Saiqa, Reefath and Shila, are deeply committed to encouraging children to value and use their different languages in the classroom and have come to this as a result of personal experience and academic study. Shila remembers how her primary school teacher used her as an interpreter for children new to the class whose English was very limited, and how proud this made her feel. Saiqa's experiences as a young learner were slightly different and she describes how she was made to feel that speaking Punjabi in the classroom was 'bad', and as a result she almost lost the ability to speak the language. She describes her own developing awareness of the need to value and nurture her own bilingualism:

> It was only after embarking on my degree that I began to challenge my personal attitude towards my mother tongue and I started to make a conscious effort to break down the language barrier which years of schooling had created between me and my parents. Only when I realised that my mother tongue deserves the same respect as any other language did I begin to have respect for my culture .... (Conteh, 2003:139)

All three teachers are aware of the constraints which surround the use of different languages in mainstream classrooms, despite its increasing support in government policy. Shila describes how she has felt uncomfortable about using her mother tongue in some school settings because she sensed a negative attitude on the part of other teachers present, both bilingual and monolingual. Fortunately, attitudes in many schools are much more positive. For example, in the school where the classes take place, the head teacher has been unfailingly welcoming and supportive of the work the teachers do.

In their work in the Saturday classes, the teachers use many of the same approaches as they use for their teaching in mainstream classes. The added dimension, as already described, is that they promote as much discussion as possible, in a range of languages. Translation has a part to play in this, and they also use a sort of 'amplification' strategy (Mercer, 2001:251), through which meanings are 'opened out' for the children. They encourage the children to extend their thinking by switching from one language to the other. Codeswitching is a distinctive feature of being bilingual, which very clearly links language, culture and identity. There is still considerable debate about its possible pedagogic benefits (Mercer, 2001:250).

For the Saturday class teachers, codeswitching is something which comes naturally and, they believe, affords an added dimension to their teaching. For example, Saiqa, whose work is described in detail below, feels that when she is able to codeswitch in her teaching, things flow easier and she is able to express her meanings more easily. We urgently need to know much more about the complex ways in which teachers and learners use codeswitching in multilingual classrooms, and complementary learning settings are rich contexts from which to gain evidence.

An example of classroom interaction

To illustrate the teachers' strategies, I present here an example of interaction between Saiqa and a group of pupils. In the discussion which follows, I focus on Saiqa's own viewpoints on the interaction between herself and her pupils and draw out her perceptions of what the extract reveals about her pedagogic decisions, her expertise and professional identity.

The whole lesson lasted for about an hour and involved the children in various Maths activities with both Saiqa and Reefath. In the short extract transcribed below, Saiqa is playing a game with twelve Year Five and Six children (10-11 year olds). There are two teams. Each has to nominate four numbers between two and twelve, which are written on the whiteboard. The teams then take turns to throw the two dice and the numbers on the board are eliminated according to the totals of the spots on the dice. Saiqa begins by asking the children to decide which numbers to write on the board. All the children are Mirpuri Punjabi speakers, so all can fully understand and participate in the codeswitching. Several of the children also speak other Pakistani languages such as Pushto and Hinko.

The lesson was videoed and then extracts were transcribed. The teachers helped with the transcription and translation of the Mirpuri Punjabi sections, and they were then checked with other Punjabi speakers. I have tried to represent the views of all the participants in this process in the discussion below.

> (Words spoken in Mirpuri Punjabi are in **bold**, with an interpretation following in <italics>.
>
> Words spoken in English are in plain text.
>
> Relevant actions are given in square brackets.
>
> Children's names have been changed.)

01 Saiqa: The smallest number I can get is 1 and 1 and 1 is **doh**
02   *<two>* .. isn't it? **Saraya nal bara namber kai?** *<What is*
03   *the biggest number you can get?>*

04 Ayisha: **Baraa** *<twelve>*

05 Saiqa: **Baraa .. thako Ayisha sunee peeay na** *<Twelve .. look,*
06   *Ayisha is listening, isn't she?>* **Baraa** *<Twelve>...*
07   because if I throw this dice, the two dice together, I can
08   get six and six, can't I? If I add them together **chay tay**
09   **chay melo thay baraa** *<six and six makes twelve>*. You
10   are going to think of four numbers .. **chaar namber ..**
11   **koi vee meeki chaar deyo .. jaray doh thay baraa nai**
12   **darmeyan nah** *<four numbers .. can you give me four*
13   *numbers which are between two and twelve?>*

14 Farhat: **Jamah karsa?** *<Are we adding?>*

15 Saiqa: **Jamah karsa .. meeki namber deyo** *<Are we adding..*
16   *give me a number>* .. give me a number .. **doh namber**
17   **deyo doh hay baraa cha darmeyan nah** *<give me two*
18   *numbers between two and twelve>*

19 Farhat: **Paanj** *<Five>*

20 Saiqa: **Paanj** *<Five>* [writes on whiteboard] **Tariq, thu meeki**
21   **ik aur namber deyo jara doh thay baraa cha**
22   **darmeyan** *<Tariq, you give me one more number between*
23   *two and twelve>* That is between two and twelve .. **Koi**
24   **vee namber deyo doh thay** ... *<Can you give me a*
25   *number between two and ...>*

26 Tariq: Four

27 Saiqa: **Chaar ... shabash!** *<Four .. good!>* [writes on
28   whiteboard] Saeed?

29 Saeed: **Daas** *<Ten>*

30 Saiqa: **Daas ..** [writes on whiteboard] **Rubi .. thu meeki ik**
31   **namber dey** *<Ten .. Rubi .. you give me a number>*

32 Rubi: **Chaay** *<Six>*

33 Saiqa: [writes on whiteboard] OK .. right .. **Ay thusa nay**
34   **chaar namber oh gayna .. paanj .. four .. daas .. thay**
35   **chay .. un me apnay chaar namber liksa** *<These are*
36   *your four numbers, five, (four), ten and six I am going to*
37   *write my four numbers>* I'm going to write my (three)
38   numbers, I'm going to put **...thray .. saath .. aat thay**
39   **yaara** *<three, seven, eight and eleven>* [writes on

40		whiteboard] **ai maaray namber ay nah .. teek kay**
41		*<these are my numbers .. okay>* **Parveen .. thu dice saat**
42		*<Parveen .. you throw the dice>* [child throws dice]
43		Parveen has thrown **chaay thay paanj .. chaay thay**
44		**paanj ...jamah karah ... kitney**
45		**banay?** *<six and five .. six and five ... what is the total?>*
46	Asif:	**Yaara** *<Eleven>*
47	Saiqa:	**Thay yaara koi ne ai nah?** [pointing to numbers written on whiteboard] *<There isn't eleven, is there?>*
48	Asif:	No
49	Saiqa:	So Parveen can't cross any numbers out, can she? I am
50		going to pretend these are Parveen's and these are my
51		numbers [pointing to numbers on the whiteboard, then
52		throwing the dice]**paanj thay chaar jamah karah .. ay**
53		**kitney banay nah?** *<five plus four totals what?>*
54	Tariq:	**Noh** *<Nine>*
55	Saiqa:	**Noh .. marai kol noh ay nah?** *<Nine .. have I got a nine*
56		*here?>*
57	Tariq:	No
58	Saiqa:	No .. so you take it in turns to play that.

Though the interaction was clearly teacher-led, most children spoke at least once, and all listened intently to the interaction. From an observer's viewpoint, they all appeared to be attentive and participated in the activity with enthusiasm. The codeswitching was fluid, with more or less equal distribution of English and Mirpuri Punjabi and no sense of dissonance between the two languages, or of one being valued over the other. As can be seen from the transcript, there is very little direct translation or repetition between the two languages, but several examples of the kind of amplification which Mercer describes, such as between lines 09 and 13 where Saiqa moves between Punjabi and English to develop her discussion of the number operations the children need to do. She uses both languages for a range of pedagogic purposes, such as giving instructions (eg lines 20-25, 41-45) and offering praise, though in Punjabi the praise is often embedded in the tone rather than the specific words, so is not easy to identify in a written transcript.

Saiqa said that she had an explicit intention to develop the children's confidence in Punjabi, She pointed out that one of her specific aims in activities such as the one described above was to model various sentence structures in Punjabi for the children which they might not have heard before. Her intention was not that they repeat her examples by rote, but that they begin to generate similar utterances of their own. She pointed to lines 02-03, 10-13, 15-18 and 43-45 in the transcript as examples of the kind of 'mathematical Punjabi' she was hoping the children would be able to develop. She clearly had some success in this, as can be seen by the way several children use Punjabi numbers, and Farhat, in line 14, interjects with his own question.

Saiqa said that she felt very relaxed about using both languages, and that she found it easier in some ways than teaching in English only. She could use whichever language came more easily as the discourse progressed. She felt that she did not really make conscious moment-by-moment decisions about when to switch from one to the other, but that she had decided on a few key purposes and kept those in mind, and they seemed intuitively to trigger the switches. She wanted to give both languages equal status in her teaching, and clearly manages to do this, as can be seen by the way the children follow her lead in the use of their mother tongue.

What about the children and their parents?

Though the children in the activity described above were clearly enjoying the bilingual Maths activity, their attitudes towards their mother tongue and their own bilingualism are not always so positive. When the classes began, many of the children were reluctant to use other languages than English, and it has taken care and patience on the part of the teachers to encourage them to do this. Their bilingualism was not something they had been led to value or regard as a positive asset in their learning in mainstream school. One boy, when asked if he had heard the word 'bilingual' before, said that he thought it had something to do with 'support' – he has clearly recognised the low status of language diversity in the particular mainstream classroom contexts he inhabits. As they have spent more time in the classes, however, the children's attitudes seem to have become much more positive. In informal interviews with me, the children talked about how they enjoyed using Punjabi with their Saturday class teachers, and how they would like to do it in 'proper' school. They are keenly aware of the social and cultural importance of their home languages within their own communities, but also perceive that, on the whole, they are not recognised and valued in mainstream school.

Currently, we do not have any real evidence of the effects of bilingual teaching on children's performance and achievements in mainstream schools in England. This is another area where detailed research is vital. In the interviews, I asked the children if they could think of any ways in which their knowledge of Punjabi informed what they did in their work in school, and one girl, in Year Two, described in some detail how her knowledge of the numbers in Punjabi helped her to count on in fives from 45 to 85 to solve a problem her teacher had given her. She explained how she counted in Punjabi in her head while she said the numbers 45, 55, 65 and so on out loud in English. She was able to articulate with impressive self-awareness the way she processed both languages simultaneously to reach the required answer. More evidence of bilingual processing like this is needed to help us to understand more fully the ways in which children can manage their own learning with all the languages in their repertoires, given the right support by their teachers.

An important theme that emerged from talking with the children, and later with some of their parents, was of the social and cultural importance of different languages to the families' lives. There was universal recognition of the importance of English and that this was, and rightly should be, the key concern of mainstream schools. But the parents I interviewed saw no contradiction between this and their active commitment to maintaining the use of other languages at home and in the community, 'We are a bilingual household,' declared one mother, who went on to say that it had given her 5-year-old son a great deal of confidence to hear his Saturday class teacher speak in Punjabi. 'He needs that kind of role model,' she concluded. She clearly saw a link between complementary and mainstream learning in the way her son was able to speak much more confidently to his mainstream teacher, after he had attended the Saturday classes for a few weeks. This confidence she attributed to the way he had been able to join in with activities much more easily in the complementary context, and then carry this over into the mainstream.

Some conclusions

The findings from the interviews with parents and children presented here are very tentative, but they reinforce the evidence from the Saturday classes of the potential of a bilingual approach to learning. They give us tantalising glimpses of the ways in which language, culture and identity play out in schools and classrooms and in wider communities, showing how even the youngest children can be aware of negative attitudes towards their home languages and cultures in the education system and wider society. But, despite the anxieties of many of our powerful politicians and policy-makers, the interviews, as well as the classroom data, show us that there are many advantages to being bilingual, and that there is nothing intrinsically problematic about using different languages simultaneously in different contexts.

Twenty years ago, Fitzpatrick (1987) offered us an open door to success for pupils who brought other languages besides English to their classrooms. Perhaps the most important finding of the MOTET project, conducted in Bradford in the early 1980s, was that ethnic minority pupils who had the opportunities to learn bilingually when they began school developed greater self-confidence as learners; their potential for success was enhanced. An important key to this success is held by their teachers.

The work of the teachers in the bilingual Saturday classes is still in its very early stages, but the potential is very exciting. It is beginning to provide evidence, such as that found in complementary classes described in other chapters in this book, of the ways in which codeswitching and other bilingual strategies can be valuable classroom approaches to learning. Perhaps even more importantly their work shows the importance of teachers having the space and the scope to develop their professional identities in ways that include their full language and cultural knowledge and capabilities. This is surely one of the routes to empowerment implied in Cummins' 'negotiating identities' model of teaching and learning, and one of the ways to achieve Ross's aspiration that 'each individual' in the education system is 'empowered' by having their 'full cultural set acknowledged and valued'.

Finding out more about the skills and knowledge of bilingual teachers has both theoretical and practical implications for education in a culturally and linguistically diverse society. It will help us to understand more fully the interconnected roles of language, culture and identity in learning and teaching, and will inform the development of more inclusive models of teacher professionalism and education. Perhaps the time is about to come when we can move through the open door, and bilingual teachers are the ones best able to show us the way.

I wish to acknowledge the help of Shila Begum, Reefath Rehman and Saiqa Riasat in the preparation of this chapter.

8

Reflections and Suggestions
for Ways Forward

Jill Bourne

This is an important book, bringing together as it does stories of children's learning and teachers' practices in a variety of types of out-of-hours community run classes and, perhaps for the first time, relating these to learning and teaching in mainstream schools. It can be mined for real life examples of bilingual language use in action, and the ways in which bilingual and multilingual children experience languages and literacies in their everyday lives.

However, the real focus of this volume is on learning, and the book makes a strong case for the contribution of complementary schools to enhanced learning. For many mainstream educationalists, this approach will be an attractive emphasis rather than the perception of out-of-hours community run classes as places solely of heritage language learning and cultural maintenance, unconnected to the mainstream educational experience.

Reading these chapters, teachers can see the ways in which community run classes already impact on children's learning, and begin to explore the possibilities for creating even greater impact through making connections in their own classes. Examining the practices of these schools and classes should also help us to critically re-examine the practices of the mainstream from a new perspective, and help to counter the monolingual lenses through which we consider what is and is not possible in school.

I should like to begin by contextualising my own response to the chapters. Like many teachers, I was aware that a number of children in my classes attended out-of-hours community run classes when I was teaching in an inner city school in the late 1970s. I talked to the children about their lessons, and many took pleasure in showing me examples of the sort of work they did. So I was aware that they had experience of different forms of literacy and pedagogy, although at that time we did not have the benefit of access to the range of narratives about children's experiences of multiliteracies that are published today, including those I have enjoyed reading in this book. However, it did not occur to me – or perhaps I was unsure of my welcome, then – to seek out and step over the threshold of my students' other classes, in order to build on their learning.

It was only later, in the 1980s, that I made my first visits to what were then called community language classes. This was as part of a national study of LA provision for bilingual pupils (Bourne, 1989), when I had the privilege of attending a range of classes involving different languages in a number of areas across England. My focus at that time was on how local authorities were supporting such classes, financially, with material resources or by making school premises available to them. In the course of this work I talked to many community run class teachers but, although I visited classes, I made no systematic observations of the activities and interactions taking place there.

Later again, as a member of the executive committee of the National Council for Mother Tongue Teaching (NCMTT), I learnt more about the classes from the perspectives of the teachers and parents involved, their aims and the level of external support desired, as they perceived these themselves. As might be expected, there was a great diversity of positions, as much within as between language groups, it should be stressed. Mainstream support was welcome, but often bought at a price – what was for some an unacceptable level of control and imposed uniformity of regulation. For others, support and recognition outweighed these disadvantages.

I am not aware of systematic studies being conducted at that time on what was actually taking place within community run classes. Research was being carried out on the organisational structures, however. The Linguistic Minorities Project (1985) mapped the extent of the organisation of classes within six regions of England. They reported eighteen different languages regularly being taught in established community funded classes, including a number of South Asian languages, and some languages of the then European Union, as well as Turkish, Chinese, Latvian, Ukranian, Polish, and Hebrew. Over 70 per cent of the learners, however, were in South Asian language classes at that time. LMP also outlined a history, showing that the earliest of the existing classes were founded in 1904, for Hebrew. The earliest recorded South Asian language classes were founded in the 1950s, being joined by more during the 1970s and 1980s.

LMP reported a range of different aims given by those running the classes. Examples included 'maintenance of identity and culture' (a Ukranian school) through a focus on writing, reading and speaking (Punjabi), 'language, culture and history' (Spanish), 'the principles of our religion, history and language' (Hebrew), 'mother-tongue, folk dances, music, religion and some school subjects' (Turkish). Different aims were presented by teachers also working in mainstream schools: 'help to learn English more effectively' was one such answer, others were 'improve exam results' and 'understand pupils' problems, link home and school'.

It is important to note this diversity of aims and the very different foci given to the classes by different community groups. It is also important to recognise the diversity *within* groups, and the different motivations which individual parents continue to have for sending their children to such classes today (see, for example, the study of Brazilian mothers and their children in London by de Souza, 2006).

In English schools, as this book points out in different ways, we have long tended to have a deficit model of bilingualism, conflating it with a need for 'English as a second language' support. We have had less awareness of the tragedy of children growing up unable to read and write in the languages they share with their parents and grandparents. I also remember one senior education adviser of South Asian family origin telling me of his shame that he could not address a gathering of his community members in their home language because his parents had switched to English 'to support his education' when he was 5 years old, so that he was now afraid that in speaking Gujerati he would be inadvertently using the language of the nursery!

For many bilingual children, perhaps most, as we see in the chapters of this volume, English has become the stronger of their languages and, in response, community run classes have had to range from those providing no more than an introduction to a 'home' or 'heritage' language to those which claim to teach the language, and go on to prepare students for GCSEs in the subject. For many community run classes, involvement in the heritage culture, manners and practices appear to be as or more important than actual language learning; in others, there is an explicit focus on complementing school learning and raising children's attainment there. Nevertheless, whether explicitly aimed at complementing and supporting mainstream educational achievement or not, what children learn in these classes will impact on their educational experience and on the values, skills and expectations they bring with them to school. In this sense, all such classes are complementary.

Globally and locally, liberal economics has led away from monolithic, single systems towards fragmentation and niche markets. Personalisation is just one way of describing the effect of modern marketing and IT services offering choices aimed at enabling the individual actively to design his or her own services. The penetration of this move into education can be seen not only in the growing diversity of types of schools, or academies, but also in recent initiatives such as the government introduction of vouchers for out-of-hours 'enrichment' classes for students identified (rather dubiously) as 'gifted and talented' – which surely should include voluntary run language classes.

In this evolving context, once out-of-hours learning gains greater acceptability, the sorts of complementary classes described in this book may seem less unusual to teachers than in the past. While out-of-school classes (apart from extra-curricular activities such as swimming, dance, drama and music lessons, for example) have not been customary in the British educational scene, they are a common part of children's education in many parts of the world.

One of the inescapable themes arising from the chapters in this book is how bilingual children experience a range of languages and literacies in their everyday lives across different contexts, while their schools appear unaware of or undervalue this impressive range of metalinguistic and linguistic skills. Children are shown to be competent users of a variety of languages, registers and scripts, unerring in matching each to its appropriate context. Some of the classes show an admirable ability to respond to the role of local vernaculars alongside standard language teaching, making educational use of code-switching and mixing.

These are powerful examples and powerful stories. However, from a research perspective, one is left asking: How do these differing classes influence the many children who attend them? What kinds of effects do the range of modes, as shown in the selected examples in this book, have on different learners and on their different stages of learning? And, indeed, are there any children who resist incorporation into complementary classes, as there are some who resist mainstream schooling?

What has been overdue – and this book goes some way towards making up for it – are clear-eyed ethnographic studies of just what such classes do offer, and the range of responses to them. For example, which types of classes have a greater impact on mainstream academic achievement? What else are children learning there which we might not have expected them to learn? Of course, community run classes vary, and what is needed is more research into the whole context of voluntary, community provision. It is time to go beyond a romantic multiculturalism and connect these schools and classes with what is known about children's learning in general, and examine them through various theoretical and pedagogical lenses.

Ellsworth (1997) suggests we ask of any teaching context, 'Who is being addressed by this pedagogy?' That is, 'What Subject position is being offered to students to imagine themselves as being and enacting?' Where there is a shift in mode of address, for example between languages, what difference does this shift make in constructing the ideal listener/student? She claims that what makes a difference to learning is not so much what is taught, or how it is taught, but *who* it is that the interaction offers students 'to imagine themselves as being or enacting' (p40). This is an intriguing suggestion, and opens up a rich vein of inquiry for researchers in the field of bilingual learning.

Elsworth also argues convincingly that teaching is not so much about dealing with a lack of knowledge, as with overcoming learners' resistance to appropriating knowledge: 'It is not a simple lack of information but the incapacity – or the refusal – to acknowledge one's own implication in the information' (p79). How far might bilingual strategies – different modes of address – which are successful in overcoming resistance and opening opportunities for learning in one context, translate into another, different, culturally and linguistically mixed context, such as the mainstream classroom? And what would the impact be on learner identity in the new context? Might a bilingual approach mean a child could see the implications for herself in what is being taught more clearly? Following Hey (1997:137):

> We urgently need to interrogate which forms of discourse create what sort of places and how these positions encode cultural and social powers for their speakers and forms of powerlessness for those silenced.

Equally powerful in this book are the examples of mainstream teachers and complementary class teachers' differing expectations and perspectives on children as learners. Robertson (Chapter Three) shows how children are positioned very differently by the way in which these expectations are materially realised in the different practices of three settings, where the same child may be positioned in one context as independent and disciplined (the mosque school); as a successful participant in joint practice (the Urdu club) and as of low ability (the mainstream classroom). I would like to read more research working to uncover the modes of address and the practices that achieve these different forms of positioning, and the ways that the children operate as active agents in their own positioning across different contexts.

There are challenges in plenty for accepted concepts of good practice in the chapters of this book, not only in terms of the way in which bilingual instructors are able to draw on two or more languages to establish and consolidate concepts in negotiation with students, but in terms of the range of pedagogical strategies in use in the different contexts. An important and interesting theme emerging from the book is the challenge to the dominant myth that pedagogies in community run schools are more traditional than those in mainstream schools. Indeed, it is suggested here that the opposite is the case, a position maintained by Mirza and Reay (2000). With children having different levels of language experience and home backgrounds, all these schools are mixed ability schools. The mainstream, which has always had so much difficulty in organising for mixed ability, may learn from examining the different ways in which they operate in these contexts (see especially Robertson, Chapter Three in this volume).

Learning about difference is not just learning about the other, in this case for educationalists better to understand complementary school processes, but also for ensuring that difference should challenge the self, that is, majority assumptions and practices. Otherwise exploring difference is no more than opening new areas for mainstream surveillance and control. In this context, the discussion in Jean Conteh's paper (Chapter Seven) of the impact on the professional identities and experiences of mainstream trained bilingual teachers working in both mainstream and complementary school contexts provides room for reflexive critique of mainstream practice and new food for thought in this area. Above all, the examples draw attention to the role of pedagogy in building cultural and learner identity – whether of the majority, within an unquestioned 'monolingual habitus' (Gogolin, 1994), or of a heritage culture, or offering more fluid, flexible and changing identities for learners recognised to be bi- or multilingual.

At the same time, the effects of globalised neo-liberalism should make us wary of assuming the extent of the impact of attending such classes on children's identity formation. Recent work by de Souza (2003, 2006) offers an interesting exploration of this issue in relation to the varied language affiliations of Brazilian children in London. Just what cultures are transmitted and acquired in the interactions, what identities constructed within particular forms of complementary, community run classes remains a matter for detailed ethnographic work.

Another major theme worthy of note in this book is the discussion of the roles of parents and community in supporting the development of successful learner identities through complementary schooling and in helping to raise attainment in mainstream school. Chen (Chapter Four) finds Chinese parents in despair at the low expectations they felt teachers had of their children. In research carried out for the Open University with parents of Pakistani, Bangladeshi and African-Caribbean family origin (Blair and Bourne, 1998) we found similar perspectives. Parents told us, for example:

> The expectation is low. Because they are different cultures or they are from third world countries, they are expected to be down the ladder somewhere.

> Usually when I go to Parents' Evenings and that, they are always saying, 'Oh yes, he has done so well and done this and that'. But the work I see, I know he can do better than that, yet he is not being pushed further, half the time he is just left to get on with it.

Low expectations and a lack of commitment by the system to their children were dominant perspectives of bilingual parents, far outweighing concerns about language support or home/heritage language teaching.

Following from this, it is important to relate the work on complementary classes in this book to the research that has been carried out on the experience of Black supplementary schools in England. Black supplementary schools, like the complementary schools of the linguistic minorities discussed in this volume, are mainly self-funded grassroots organisations. Mirza and Reay (2000) identified more than 60 such schools operating across fifteen London boroughs, with twelve in Lambeth alone.

These schools explicitly set out to build the confidence and self-respect of students alongside a determined effort to raise levels of academic achievement in the mainstream school curriculum. Drawing on ethnographic data from four supplementary schools, Mirza and Reay (2000) suggest that the role of Black supplementary schools is not merely complementary, but rather 'radical and subversive' (p521), acting as 'a covert social movement for educational change', despite their 'quiet conformist exterior' (*ibid*). They quote one supplementary school teacher as saying:

> I think one of the things we really succeed in is giving the children a positive sense of self. We help them feel comfortable with their blackness when out there they are bound to come up against situations in which they are made to feel uncomfortable about being black. (Mirza and Reay, 2000:532)

Mirza and Reay argue that these supplementary schools generate oppositional meanings, decentring the assumptions of mainstream schooling and
providing 'parallel discursive arenas where members of subordinated social
groups invent and circulate counter discourses, which in turn permit them to
formulate oppositional interpretations of their identities, interests and needs'
(Fraser, 1994: 84; quoted in Mirza and Reay, 2000:532).

Drawing on the concepts developed by Mirza and Reay offers another way of
viewing the complementary schools described in this book, seeing them as
implicitly acting to counter the normative monolingualism of the mainstream school by valorising bilingualism. Just as the Black supplementary
school 'provided their black pupils with familiarity and a sense of centrality
often missing from their experience of mainstream schooling' (Mirza and
Reay, 2000: 533), so also bilingual complementary schools offer a 'safe space'
(Martin *et al*, Chapter Six in this volume) for exploring and inventing bilingual
identities. For if, as Gillborn (1995) argues, 'blackness' is constructed 'at best
as marginal, at worst as pathological' (quoted in Mirza and Reay, 2000:533)
then, we might argue, so is bilingualism equally pathologised in England today. This suggests the importance of finding permissible and positive places
from which minorities are enabled to speak to their children.

Thus, as with the black supplementary schools, complementary schools provide alternative and autonomous spaces, where 'oppositional and empowering narratives' of identity can be created for the communities involved. In
these schools 'rewriting blackness as a positive social identity' (Mirza and
Reay, 2000:534), there is space for rewriting bilingualism and, indeed, multilingualism as offering a positive, even powerful, way of being.

This suggests, too, that in shifting perspective from researching community
led classes with a focus on language learning to a focus on wider pedagogic
outcomes for learners as defined by mainstream schooling, research should
not lose sight of community based classes as a means of maintaining the vitality of the languages of minority ethnic groups within the UK, nor of their pro-
ductive work in offering flexible and hybrid identities – such extra schools and
classes having an important role of their own. As Burbules (2000) has argued,
we should not 'domesticate' difference, to make it safe and easily compre-
hensible from majority standpoints. After all, difference is defined by resistance to dominant norms and challenges these.

For many complementary classes, aims go beyond academic learning to
insertion into particular linguistic and cultural practices and value systems
which may not be shared with the dominant society. This leads me to the con-

clusion that there may be things happening in community run schools that could not happen in the mainstream as, indeed, there may be things happening there which, if brought into the mainstream, would simply not be the same. As Moss (2001) has shown, home practices are necessarily transformed when brought into the school context, and this would hold similarly for complementary school practices where these were not developed on mainstream school lines. Calling for closer links between mainstream and community run classes does not mean the replacement of one by the other, nor indeed the surveillance and control of such classes by mainstream education agents.

The Swann Report (DES, 1985) is often criticised, as it has been in this volume (Chapter One), for recommending that communities should continue to be responsible for the teaching of the mother tongue through community based classes. It needs to be noted, however, that this decision was reached in part through the representations of community organisations to the Committee. Many community organisations were concerned that receiving government funding would mean government control of their curriculum and practices, turning their classes into pseudo-mainstream classes rather than alternatives and limiting their options in working with children (Bourne, 1989).

On the matter of incorporating mother tongue teaching into mainstream schools themselves, there were mixed feelings. There was among some a fear, justified in part by history, that making separate provision for children from minority language groups would lead to them being pulled out of mainstream provision, not given access to the sort of provision which is enjoyed by the children of those most successful and established in society, set aside in what would come to be seen as second class schooling.

Clearly, if communities and parents do not feel fully involved in the democratic development of education policy, there remains this suspicion. I write this in full awareness of this fear, here at my desk on study leave in South Africa. Colonial education policy in Africa tended towards vernacular education for the native population, where only the children of the elite bought themselves into an English education. The apartheid years in South Africa strengthened the resistance to education in languages other than English, again seen as a way of denying access to employment opportunities and higher education.

Today, despite a supportive national policy towards mother tongue education, the majority of South African parents struggle to enrol their children in English medium schools to avoid their placement in other language streams which are seen as being second class. It seems clear that it is not only that English is seen as providing social mobility, but that the motivations of those offering separate language streams are questioned: people still simply do not believe that the schools are committed to raising standards and ensuring high levels of academic success for their children. Separate language streams are viewed in post-apartheid South Africa, with some justification, as an attempt by the economic elite to exclude and marginalise some sections of society, to the benefit of their own children.

Without real involvement and trust, minority groups in Europe may have similar perceptions. In this context, while there is clearly much more that many schools with significant numbers of particular language speakers could do in teaching the language as a curriculum subject, there will remain a genuine niche for continuing community designed and run voluntary classes, developing their own curriculum and forms of pedagogy alongside mainstream, inclusive education.

This should also remind us that research on community run classes, unless with the close participation of the participants, might lead to similar distrust. There is a real need carefully to consider the ethics of research in this field, so that researchers do not inadvertently expose community run classes to greater surveillance and control by government and other agencies, without ensuring that minority perspectives have space in their reports to challenge dominant ideologies on pedagogy, curriculum and child-rearing practices.

I remember a Chinese language support teacher working in a London primary school once telling me of his struggle, on coming to England from teaching in Hong Kong, to understand the English system and particularly its common classroom practices. He said that he had come to understand his role as a teacher more clearly through learning about the contrasts between different cultures of pedagogy, and had thereby gained a grasp of a wider range of strategies for meeting children's varied needs. This needs to be a two-way experience, and there must be a similar effect on teachers who read this book, encouraging a desire to know more, to explore new ways of supporting bilingual approaches to learning, and to reappraise dominant perceptions of good practice in the light of their students' experiences as members of a complex global society.

References

Abdelrazak, M (2001) *Towards more effective Supplementary and Mother-tongue Schools (in England).* London: Resource Unit for Supplementary and Mother-tongue Schools

Abreu, G and Lambert, H (2003) *The Education of Portuguese Students in England and Channel Islands Schools.* Luton: Department of Psychology, University of Luton

Adams, MJ (1990) *Beginning to Read: new phonics in context.* Oxford: Heinemann

Agar, M (2005) Local discourse and global research: the role of local knowledge, *Language in Society* 34(1) p1-22

Arthur, J (2003) Baro Afkaaga Hooyo! A case study of Somali literacy teaching in Liverpool. *International Journal of Bilingual Education and Bilingualism.* 6(3-4) p253-266

Arthur, J and Martin, PW (2006) Accomplishing lessons in postcolonial classrooms: comparative perspectives from Botswana and Brunei Darussalam. *Comparative Education* 42(2) p177-202

Baetens Beardsmore, H (2003) Who is afraid of bilingualism? In J-M Dewaele, A Housen and Li Wei (eds) *Bilingualism: Beyond Basic Principles.* Clevedon: Multilingual Matters

Baker, C (2001) *Foundations of Bilingual Education and Bilingualism (3rd edition).* Clevedon: Multilingual Matters

Barradas, O (1993) A study of the oral language of Portuguese bilingual children in London. Unpublished MA dissertation. Institute of Education, University of London

Barradas, O (1996) A study of the oral proficiency of Portuguese bilingual children in London. In T Cline and N Frederikson (eds) *Curriculum Related Assessment, Cummins and Bilingual Children.* Cleveland: Multilingual Matters

Barradas, O (2004) Portuguese students in London schools: Patterns of participation in community language classes and patterns of educational achievement. Unpublished doctoral dissertation. Goldsmiths College, University of London

Barrantes, R (2005) Analysis of ICT demand. In J Mariscal and H Galperin (eds) *Digital Poverty: Latin American and Caribbean Perspectives.* Regional Dialogue on Information Society (DIRSI). Online book. http://www.dirsi.net/index.php?module=htmlpages&func=display&pid=63

Basic essentials for Muslims. (no date) Unpublished document

Basic principles of Islam. (no date). Slough: Free Islamic Book Service

Beykont, ZF (1994) Academic progress of a non-dominant group: a longitudinal study of Puerto Ricans in New York City's late-exit bilingual programs. Unpublished doctoral dissertation. Graduate School of Education, Harvard University

Bhachu, P (1985) *Parental Education Strategies: the case of Punjabi Sikhs in Britain.* Centre for Research in Ethnic Relations, University of Warwick

Bhatt, A (1994) Gujarati literacies in Leicester. *RaPAL Bulletin 25*, p3-9

Bhatt, A and Martin-Jones, M (1992) Whose resource? Minority languages, bilingual learners and language awareness. In N Fairclough (ed) *Critical Language Awareness.* London: Longman (p285-302)

Bhatt, A, Barton, D and Martin-Jones, M (1994) Gujarati literacies in East Africa and Leicester: changes in social identities and multilingual practices. *Working Paper Series No 56.* University of Lancaster: Centre for Language in Social Life

Bhatt, A, Bhojani, N, Creese, A and Martin, P W (2004) Complementary and mainstream schooling: a case for reciprocity. *Occasional Paper* 18. NALDIC

Bhatti, FM (1978) Young Pakistanis in Britain. Educational needs and problems. *New Community* 6(3)

Blackledge, A (2004) Constructions of identity in political discourse in multilingual Britain. In A Pavlenko and A Blackledge (eds.) *Negotiation of Identities in Multilingual Contexts* Clevedon: Multilingual Matters (p68-92)

Blair, M and Bourne, J (1998) Making the difference: teaching and learning in successful multilingual schools. *Research Report* 59. London: DFES

Blunkett, D (2002) Integration with diversity: globalisation and the renewal of democracy and civil society. In P Griffith and M Leonard (eds) *Reclaiming Britishness.* London: The Foreign Policy Centre (p65-77)

Boaler, J, Wiliam, D and Brown, M (2000) Students' experiences of ability grouping – disaffection, polarisation and the construction of failure. *British Educational Research Journal* 26(5) p631-648

Bourne, J (1989) *Moving into the Mainstream: LEA provision for bilingual pupils in England and Wales.* Windsor: NFER-Nelson

Bourne, J (1997) 'The grown-ups know best': language policy making in Britain in the 1990s. In W Eggington and H Wren (eds) *Language Policy: Dominant English Pluralist Challenges.* Amsterdam: John Benjamins (p49-65)

Bourne, J (2001) Discourses and identities in a multi-lingual primary classroom. *Oxford Review of Education* 27(1) p103-114

Broady, M (1955) The social adjustment of Chinese immigrants in Liverpool. *Sociological Review* 3, p65-75

Bruner, JS (1996) *The Culture of Education.* Cambridge, Mass., Harvard University Press

Bryant, P and Bradley, L (1985) *Children's Reading Problems.* Oxford: Blackwell

Burbules, N (2000) The limits of dialogue as a critical pedagogy. In P Trifonas (ed) *Revolutionary Pedagogies.* London: Routledge (p251-273)

Callender, C (1997) *Education for Empowerment: the practice and philosophies of black teachers.* Stoke-on-Trent: Trentham Books

Carle, E (1992) *The Very Hungry Caterpillar* (English and Gujerati edition). London: Mantra

Carrington, V and Luke, A (1997) Literacy and Bourdieu's sociological theory: a reframing. *Language and Education* 11(2) p96-112

Cazden, C, John, VP, and Hymes, D (eds) (1972) *Functions of Language in the Classroom.* New York: Teachers' College Press

Central Advisory Council for England (1967) *Children and their Primary Schools* (The Plowden Report) London: HMSO

Chau, R and Yu, S (2001) Social exclusion of Chinese people in Britain. *Critical Social Policy* 21(1) p103-125

Chen, Y (2007) Equality and inequality of opportunity in education: Chinese bilingual children in the English mainstream classroom. *Language Culture and Curriculum* 20(1) p36-51

Cheng, Y and Heath, A (1993) Ethnic origins and class destinations. *Oxford Review of Education* 19(2) p151-65

Chevannes, F and Reeves, M (1987) The Black voluntary school movement. In B Troyna, (ed) *Racial Inequality in Education.* London: Tavistock. (p147-169)

Chun, K (1995) The myth of Asian American success and its educational ramifications. In DT Nakanishi and TY Nishida (eds) *The Asian American Educational Experience: a source book for teachers and students.* New York: Routledge

Clay, M (1975) *Young Fluent Readers.* London: Heinemann

Coard, B (1971) *How the West Indian Child is made Educationally Sub-Normal in the British School System.* London: New Beacon Books

Cole, M (1985) The zone of proximal development: where culture and cognition create each other. In JV Wertsch (ed) *Culture, Communication and Cognition: Vygotskyan Perspectives.* New York: Cambridge University Press (p146-161)

Cole, M (1996) *Cultural Psychology: a once and future discipline.* Cambridge, Mass: The Belknap Press of Harvard University Press

Conteh, J (2003) *Succeeding in Diversity: culture, language and learning in primary classrooms.* Stoke-on-Trent: Trentham Books

Conteh, J (2006a) Widening the inclusion agenda: policy, practice and language diversity in the curriculum In R Webb (ed) *Changing Teaching and Learning in the Primary School.* Buckingham: Open University Press (p128-138)

Conteh, J (ed) (2006b) *Promoting Learning for Bilingual Pupils 3-11: opening doors to success.* London: Sage Publications

Conteh, J (2007) Opening doors to success in multilingual classrooms: Bilingualism, code-switching and the professional identities of 'ethnic minority' primary teachers, *Language and Education,* 21(6)

Creese, A (2005) *Teacher Collaboration and Talk in Multilingual Classrooms.* Clevedon: Multilingual Matters

Creese, A, Bhatt, A, Bhojani, N and Martin, P W (2006) Multicultural, heritage and learner identities in complementary schools. *Language and Education* 20(1) p23-43

Creese, A and Martin, P W (eds) (2003) *Multilingual Classroom Ecologies: Inter-relationships, Interactions and Ideologies.* Clevedon: Multilingual Matters

Cummins, J (1979) Cognitive/academic language proficiency, linguistic interdependence, the optimum age question and some other matters. *Working Papers on Bilingualism.* 19, p121-129

Cummins, J (1980) The entry and exit fallacy in bilingual education. *NABE Journal* 4, p25-60

Cummins, J (1984) *Bilingualism and Special Education: issues in assessment and pedagogy.* Clevedon: Multilingual Matters

Cummins, J (2000) *Language Power and Pedagogy: bilingual children in the crossfire.* Clevedon: Multilingual Matters.

Cummins, J (2001) *Negotiating Identities: education for empowerment in a diverse society,* 2nd edn Ontario, CA: California Association for Bilingual Education

Datta, M (2001) *Bilinguality and Literacy: principles and practice.* London: Continuum

Dave, J (1991) The Gujerati speech community. In V Edwards and S Alladina (eds) *Multilingualism in the British Isles, Vol.2: Africa, the Middle East and Asia.* London: Longman

de Souza, A (2003) *Children see language as a feature of their ethnicity.* www.naldic.org.uk/docs/BRB5.doc

de Souza, A (2006) Should I speak Portuguese or English? Ethnic and social identity construction in the language choices of Brazilian mothers and their mixed heritage children at home and in a community language school in the UK. Unpublished PhD thesis, University of Southampton

DES (Department of Education and Science) (1975) *A Language for Life.* The Bullock Report. London: HMSO

DES (Department of Education and Science) (1981) *West Indian Children in our Schools.* The Rampton Report. London: HMSO

DES (Department of Education and Science) (1985) *Education for All. Report of the Committee of Inquiry into the Education of Ethnic Minority Groups.* The Swann Report. London: HMSO

DES (Department of Education and Science) (1988) *Report of the Committee of Inquiry into Teaching of English Language.* The Kingman Report. London: HMSO

DfEE (Department for Education and Employment) (1998) *The National Literacy Strategy: A Framework for Teaching.* London: HMSO

DfEE (Department for Education and Employment) (1999a) *The National Curriculum Handbook for Primary Teachers in England.* London: DfEE and QCA

DfEE (Department for Education and Employment) (1999b) *The National Literacy Strategy. Supporting Students Learning English as an Additional Language.* London: DfEE

DfEE (Department of Education and Employment) (2001) *Statistics in Education: Schools in England, 2000.* London: DfEE

DfES (Department for Education and Skills) (2002a) *Ethnic Minority Achievement Grant: Analysis of LEA Action Plans.* L Tikly, A Osler, J Hill, and K Vincent, with P Andrews, J Jeffreys, T Ibrahim, C Panel and M Smith. The Graduate School of Education, University of Bristol and The Centre for Citizenship Studies in Education, University of Leicester. Research Report 371. Department for Education and Skills

DfES (Department for Education and Skills) (2002b) *Languages for All: Languages for Life. A Strategy for England.* London: DfES

DfES (Department for Education and Skills) (2003a) *Publications and Materials for Continuing Professional Development.* London: DfES

DfES (Department for Education and Skills) (2003b) *Excellence and Enjoyment: A Strategy for Primary Schools.* London: DfES Also available at: http://www.standards.dfes.gov.uk/ primary/publications/literacy/63553/

DfES (Department for Education and Skills) (2003c) *Every Child Matters; Change for Children: Making it Happen, Working Together for Children, Young People and Families.* Nottingham: DfES

DfES (Department for Education and Skills) (2003d) *Aiming High: Raising Attainment for Minority Ethnic Pupils.* London: DfES Also available at: http://www.standards.dfes.gov.uk/ midbins/ema/Aiming_High_Consultation_Doc.DOC

DfES (Department for Education and Skills) (2005a) *The Key Stage 2 Framework for Languages* http://www.standards.dfes.gov.uk/primary/features/languages/ (consulted, March 2007)

DfES (Department for Education and Skills) (2005b) *Guidance on implementation of the KS2 Framework for languages. Part II.* DfES1721-2005-EN <http://publications. teachernet.gov.uk/ eOrderingDownload/Framework%20for%20Languages%20-%20Part%202.pdf> (consulted, March 2007)

(DfES) Department for Education and Skills (2006) *Excellence and Enjoyment: Learning and Teaching for Bilingual Children in the Primary Years.* London: DfES.

Desai, N (1989) *The Raja's Big Ears.* London: Jennie Ingham Associates

DGIDC (2005) Quadro de Referência para o Ensino Português no Estrangeiro – QuaREPE. Direcção-Geral de Inovação e de Desenvolvimento Curricular Lisboa, Portugal. <http:// 213.63.132.233/epe/uploads/Quadro_de_Referencia.pdf>

(consulted, March 2007)

Dosanjh, JS (1969) Punbjabi Immigrant Children – their social and educational problems in adjustment. *Educational Paper* 10, University of Nottingham.

Drew, P (1990) Conversation analysis. In *Encyclopaedia of Language and Linguistics.* London: Pergamon

Duranti, A and Ochs, E (1996) *Syncretic Literacy: multiculturalism in Samoan-American families.* National Centre for Research on Cultural Diversity and Second Language Learning

Education Bradford (2006) *Talk across the Curriculum: An Activity Guide for 'Speaking and Listening'*

Edwards, J (1994) *Multilingualism.* London: Routledge

Edwards, V (1997) Reading in multilingual classrooms. In V Edwards and D Corson (eds) *Encyclopaedia of Language and Education. Volume 2 Literacy.* Dordrecht: Kluwer Academic Publishers

Edwards, V (2001) Community languages in the United Kingdom. In G Extra and D Gorter (eds) *The Other Languaes of Europe: Demographic, Sociolinguistic and Educational Perspectives.* Clevedon: Multilingual Matters (p243-260)

Edwards, V (2005) *Multilingualism in the English-Speaking World.* Oxford: Blackwell

Edwards, V and Redfern, A (1992) *The World in a Classroom. language in education in Britain and Canada.* Clevedon: Multilingual Matters

Ellsworth, E (1997) *Teaching Positions: difference, pedagogy and the power of address.* London and NY: Teachers' College Press

EEC (European Communities Council) (1977) *Council Directive on the Education of Children of Migrant Workers. 77/486/EEC*

Fairclough, N (2003) *Analysing Discourse: textual analysis for social research.* London: Routledge

Fishman, J (1989) *Language and Ethnicity in Minority Sociolinguistic Perspective.* Clevedon: Multilingual Matters

Fitzpatrick, F (1987) *The Open Door: the Bradford Bilingual Project.* Clevedon: Multilingual Matters

Francis, B and Archer, L (2005) British-Chinese pupils' constructions of the value of education. *British Educational Research Journal*, 31(1) p89-108

Freebody, P (2001) Theorising new literacies, in and out of school. *Language and Education* 15(2-3) p105-116

Gee, JP (1985) The narrativisation of experience in the oral style. *Journal of Education*, 167, p9-35

Gee, JP (1991) A linguistic approach to narrative. *Journal of Narrative and Life History*, 1(1) p15-39

Gee, JP (2005) *Introduction to Discourse Analysis 2nd edn.* London: Routledge

Ghuman, PAS (1980) Punjabi parents and English education. *Educational Research* 22(2) p121-30

Ghuman, PAS (2003) *Double Loyalties: South Asian adolescents in the west.* Cardiff: University of Wales Press

Giles, H, Bourhis, R and Taylor, DM (1977) Towards a theory of language in ethnic group relations. In H Giles (ed) *Language, Ethnicity and Intergroup Relations.* London: Academic Press

Gillborn, D (1995) *Racism and Anti-racism in Real Schools.* Buckingham: Open University Press.

Gogolin, I (1994) *Der monolinguale Habitus oder multilinguale Schule.* Munster, New York: Waxmann Verlag

Goodman, K (1969) Analysis of oral reading miscues: applied psycholinguistics. *Reading Research Quarterly* 5(1) p9-30

Goswami, U (1995) Rhyme in children's early reading. In R Beard, (ed) *Rhyme, Reading and Writing.* London: Hodder and Stoughton

Graff, HJ (1979) *The Literacy Myth: literacy and social structure in the nineteenth century city.* New York: Academic Press

Gregory, E (1993) Sweet and sour: learning to read in British and Chinese school. *English in Education,* 27(3) p53-59

Gregory, E (1994) Cultural assumptions and early years pedagogy: the effect of home culture on minority children's perceptions of reading in school. *Language, Culture and Curriculum* 7(20) p111-124

Gregory, E (1996) *Making Sense of a New World: learning to read in a second language.* London: Paul Chapman

Gregory, E (1998) Siblings as mediators of literacy in linguistic minority communities. *Language and Education* 12(1) p33-54

Gregory, E (2001) Sisters and brothers as language and literacy teachers: synergy between siblings playing and working together. *Journal of Early Childhood Literacy* 1(3) p301-322

Gregory, E, Lathwell, J, Mace, J and Rashid, N (1993) *Literacy at Home and at School*. London: Faculty of Education, Goldsmiths College

Gregory, E and Williams, A (2000a) *City Literacies: learning to read across generations and cultures*. London: Routledge

Gregory, E and Williams, A (2000b) Work or play: 'Unofficial' literacies in the lives of two East London communities. In M Martin-Jones and K Jones, (eds) *Multilingual Literacies: Reading and Writing in Different Worlds*. Amsterdam: John Benjamins Publishing Company

Gregory, E, Long, S and Volk, D (eds) (2004) *Many Pathways to Literacy: young children learning with siblings, grandparents, peers and communities*. London: RoutledgeFalmer

Gumperz, J (1982) *Discourse Strategies*. Cambridge: Cambridge University Press

Hall, KA, Özerk, K, Zulfiqar, M and Tan, JEC (2002) 'This is our school': provision, purpose and pedagogy of supplementary schooling in Leeds and Oslo. *British Educational Research Journal* 28(3) p399-418

Hamers, JF and Blanc, MHA (1989) *Bilinguality and Bilingualism*. Cambridge: Cambridge University Press

Heath, SB (1983) *Ways with Words: life and work in communities and classrooms*. Cambridge: Cambridge University Press

Heath, SB (1986) Sociocultural contexts of language development. In D Holt (ed) *Beyond Language: Social Change and Cultural Factors in Schooling Minority Students*. California State University, CA: Los Angeles Evaluation, Dissemination and Assessment Center

Heller, M (1995) Language choice, social institutions, and symbolic domination. *Language in Society* 24, p373-405

Hey, V (1997) *The Company she Keeps: an ethnography of girls' friendship*. Buckingham: Open University

HMSO (1988) *Education Reform Act*. London: HMSO

Hong-Kingston, M (1975) *The Woman Warrior*. London: Picador

Hussain, M (1982) *Study of Watford's Asian Community*. Watford: Watford Community Relations Council

Hymes, D (1974) *Foundations in Sociolinguistics: an ethnographic approach*. Philadelphia: University of Pennsylvania Press

IGE (2005) *Relatório da Visita de Inspecção ao Ensino Português no Reino Unido – 16 a 21 de Maio de 2005*. Inspecção-Geral da Educação. Lisboa, Portugal

Ireson, J and Hallam, S (1999) Raising standards: is ability grouping the answer? *Oxford Review of Education* 25(3) p343-358

Jones, D (1979) The Chinese in Britain: origins and development of a community. *New Community*, 7(3) p397-402

Jones, D (1980) Chinese Schools in Britain: a minority's response to its own need. *Trend in Education* (Spring) p15-18

Keating, MC (1990) Language Contact Between Portuguese and English: Portuguese Immigrants in London – a Case Study. Unpublished MPhil dissertation. New Hall, University of Cambridge, England

Kempadoo, M and Abdelrazak, M (1999) *Directory of Supplementary and Mother-tongue Supplementary Classes 1999-2000,* London: Resource Unit for Supplementary and Mother-tongue Schools

Kenner, C (2000a) Biliteracy in a monolingual school system? English and Gujarati in South London. *Language, Culture and Curriculum* 13(1) p13-30

Kenner, C (2000b) *Home Pages: literacy links for bilingual children.* Stoke-on-Trent: Trentham Books

Kenner, C (2004a) Living in simultaneous worlds: difference and integration in bilingual script learning. *International Journal of Bilingual Education and Bilingualism* 7(1) p43-61

Kenner, C (2004b) *Becoming Biliterate: young children learning different writing systems.* Stoke-On-Trent: Trentham Books

Khan, NA and Kabir, MA (1999) Mother-tongue education among Bangladeshi children in Swansea: an exploration. *Language Learning Journal* 20, p20-26

Lantolf, JP (ed) (2000) *Sociocultural Theory and Language Learning.* Oxford: Oxford University Press

Lambeth Education (2000) *Education Statistics 1999-2000.* London Borough of Lambeth

Leicester City Council (2006) *The diversity of Leicester: a demographic profile.* Leicester: Leicester City Council and the Leicester Partnership

Leicester City Council (2007) http://www.leicester.gov.uk/your-council—services/education—lifelong-learning/about-us/lea-services/multicultural-education/complementary-schools/partnership-working (Consulted, March 2007)

Leicestershire County Council (1991) *Ethnic Minority Groups Living in Leicestershire. Census 1991.* Leicester: Department and Planning. Leicestershire County Council

Li, G (2003) Literacy, culture, and politics of schooling: Counter-narratives of a Chinese Canadian family. *Anthropology and Education Quarterly* 34(2) p184-206

Li Wei (1993) Mother-tongue maintenance in a Chinese community school in Newcastle upon Tyne: Developing a social network perspective. *Language and Education* 7(3) p199-215

Li Wei (1994) *Three Generations, Two Languages, One Family: Language Choice and Language Shift in a Chinese Community in Britain.* Clevedon: Multilingual Matters

Li Wei (2000) Extending schools: bilingual development of Chinese children in Britain. In M Datta (ed) *Bilinguality and Literacy: principles and practice.* London: Continuum

Li Wei (2006) Complementary schools, past, present and future. *Language and Education* 20(1) p76-83

Li, H and Rao, N (2000) Parental influences on Chinese literacy development: A comparison of preschoolers in Beijing, Hong Kong and Singapore. *International Journal of Behavioural Development* 24(1) p81-90

Lin, AMY (1999) Doing-English-lessons in the reproduction or transformation of social worlds? *TESOL Quarterly* 33(3) p393-412

Linguistic Minorities Project (1985) *The Other Languages of England.* London: Routledge and Kegan Paul

MacCleod, F (1985) *Parents in Partnership – Involving Muslin parents in their Children's Education.* Coventry: Community Education Development Centre

McLean, M (1985) Private supplementary schools and the ethnic challenge of state education in Britain. In C Brock and W Tulasiewicz (eds) *Cultural Identity and Educational Policy.* London: Croom Helm (p326-345)

Martin, PW, Bhatt, A, Bhojani, N and Creese, A (2003) *Preliminary report on complementary schools and their communities in Leicester.* University of Leicester: ESRC R000223949. Also available at: http://www.uel.ac.uk/education/staff/documents/complementery_schools.pdf

Martin, PW, Creese, A, Bhatt, A and Bhojani, N (2004) *Final Report on Complementary Schools and their Communities in Leicester.* University of Leicester: ESRC R000223949. Also available at: http://www.uel.ac.uk/education/staff/finalreport.pdf

Martin, PW, Bhatt, A, Bhojani, N and Creese, A (2006) Managing bilingual interaction in a Gujarati complementary school in Leicester. *Language and Education* 20(1) p5-22

Martin-Jones, M and Bhatt, A (1998) Literacies in the lives of young Gujarati speakers in Leicester. In A Durgunoglu and L Verhoven (eds) *Literacy Development in a Multilingual Context. Cross-Cultural Perspectives.* Mahwah, NJ: Lawrence Erlbaum (p37-50)

Massey, I (1991) *More Than Skin Deep: developing anti-racist multicultural education in schools.* London: Hodder and Stoughton

Maybin, J (2003) *The potential contribution of linguistic ethnography to Vygotskyan studies of talk and learning in education* http://www.ling-ethnog.org.uk (consulted, March 2007)

Mayone-Dias, E (1986) *O Portinglês.* Peregrinação – Artes e Letras da Diáspora Portuguesa, 3(11) p4-9. Lisboa: Editora Peregrinação

Mercer, N (2001) Language for teaching a language. In C Candlin and N Mercer (eds) *English Language Teaching in its Social Context* Buckingham/Sydney: Open University/Routledge/ Macquarie University (p243-257).

Miller, J (1983) *Many Voices, Bilingualism, Culture and Education.* London: Routledge and Kegan Paul

Ministry of Education (1963) *English for Immigrants.* Ministry of Education Pamphlet Number 43. London: HMSO

Mirza, H and Reay, D (2000) Spaces and places of Black educational desire: rethinking Black supplementary schools as a new social movement. *Sociology* 34(3) p521-544

Moll, LC, Amanti, C, Neff, D and Gonzalez, N (1992) 'Funds of knowledge' for teaching: using a qualitative approach to connect homes and classrooms, *Theory into Practice*, 31(2) p132-141

Moore, A (1999) *Teaching Multicultured Students.* London: Falmer Press

Moss, G (2001) To work or play? Junior age non fiction as objects of design. *Reading, Literacy and Language* 35(3) p106-110

Mullard, C (1981) Multiracial education in Britain: from assimilation to cultural pluralism. In M Arnot (ed) *Race and Gender: equal opportunities policies in education.* Oxford: Pollard

National Association for Language Development in the Curriculum (NALDIC) (2004) www.naldic.org.uk /docs/members/documents/EALPilotDiscussionPaper.pdf. (consulted, February 2006)

National Census (2001) http://www.statistics.gov.uk/census/

Nieto, S (1999) *The Light in their Eyes: creating multicultural learning communities.* Teachers' College Press and Trentham Books

Ny, KC (1968) *The Chinese in London*. London: Oxford University Press

Ogbu, JU (1981) School ethnography: a multilevel approach. *Anthropology and Education* 12(1) p3-19

Olsen, L (1997) *An Invisible Crisis: The educational needs of Asian Pacific American youth.* New York: Asian American/ Pacific Islanders in Philanthropy

Osborne, AB (1996) Practice into theory into practice: culturally relevant pedagogy for students we have marginalised and normalised. *Anthropology and Education Quarterly* 27(3) p285-314

Pang, M (1999) The employment situation of young Chinese adults in the British labour market. *Personnel Review* 28 p41-57

Parke, T, Drury, R, Kenner, C and Robertson, LH (2002) Revealing invisible worlds: connecting the mainstream with bilingual children's home and community learning. *Journal of Early Childhood Literacy* 2(2) p195-220

Parker, D (2000) The Chinese takeaway and the diasporic habitus: space, time and power geometrics. In B Hesse (ed) *Un/settled Multiculturalisms*. London: Zed Books

Peal, E and Lambert, WE (1962) The relation of bilingualism to intelligence. In WE Lambert (ed) *Language, Psychology and Culture*. Stamford: Stanford University Press

Philips, S (1983) *The Invisible Culture: communication in classroom and community on the Warm Springs Indian Reservation*. White Plains, NY: Longman USA

Ramírez, JD (1992) Executive Summary. *Bilingual Research Journal* 16, p1-62

Rampton, B, Harris, R and Leung, C (1997) Multilingualism in England. *Annual Review of Applied Linguistics* 17, p224-241

Ran, A (2000) Learning to read and write at home: the experience of Chinese families in Britain. In M Martin-Jones and K Jones (eds) *Multilingual Literacies: reading and writing different worlds*. Amsterdam: John Benjamins

Rassool, N (1995) Language, cultural pluralism and the silencing of minority discourses in England and Wales. *Journal of Education Policy* 10(3) p287-302

Reay, D and Mirza, H (2001) Black supplementary schools: spaces of radical blackness. In: R Majors (ed) *Educating our Black Children: new directions and radical approaches*. London: RoutledgeFalmer

Reid, E, Smith, G and Morawska, A (1985) *Languages in London. Community Languages and Education Project*. London: University of London Institute of Education

Rex, J and Tomlinson, S (1979) *Colonial Immigrants in a British City: a class analysis*. London: Routledge and Kegan Paul

Robertson, LH (2004) Multilingual flexibility and literacy learning in an Urdu community school. In Gregory *et al* (2004)

Robertson, LH (2005) Teaching and learning in community language schools. *Occasional Paper* 19. National Association for Language Development in the Curriculum (NALDIC)

Robertson, LH (2006) Learning to read 'properly' by moving between parallel literacy classes. *Language and Education* 20(1) p44-61

Rosowsky, A (2001) Decoding as a cultural practice and its effects on the reading process of bilingual pupils. *Language and Education* 15(1) p56-70

Ross, A (2002) Towards a representative profession: teachers from the ethnic minorities http:// www.multiverse.ac.uk/viewArticle.aspx?contentId=446 (consulted August 2006)

Ross, T (1993) *Don't Do That!* London: Red Fox Picture Books

Saxena, M (1994) Literacies among Panjabis in Southall. In M Hamilton, D Barton and R Ivanic (eds) *Worlds of Literacy.* Clevedon: Multilingual Matters

Scribner, S (1984) Literacy in three metaphors. *American Journal of Education* 93(1) p6-21

Sham, S and Woodrow, D (1998) Chinese children and their families in England. *Research Papers in Education* 13(2) p203-226

Singh, G (2003) Multiculturalism in contemporary Britain: reflections on the 'Leicester model'. *International Journal on Multicultural Societies* 5(1) p40-54

Smith, B [1943] (2001) *A Tree Grows in Brooklyn.* New York: Harper Perennial – Modern Classic

Smith, F (1985) *Reading.* Cambridge: Cambridge University Press

Smith, D and Tomlinson, S (1989) *The School Effect: A study of multi-racial comprehensives.* London: Policy Studies Institute

Sneddon, R (1998) 'Allwrite in Hackney' *ILECC Journal* 1, p12-13

Sneddon, R (2000a) Language and literacy: children's experiences in multilingual environments. *International Journal of Bilingual Education and Bilingualism* 3(4) p265-282

Sneddon, R (2000b) Language and literacy practices in Gujarati Muslim families. In M Martin-Jones and K Jones (eds) *Multilingual Literacies.* Amsterdam: John Benjamins Publishing Co.

Sneddon, R and Patel, K (2003) The Raja's Big Ears: the journey of a story across cultures. *Language and Education* 17(5) p371-384

SOPEMI Report (1976). (Systéme d'Oservation Permanente des Migrations) Relatório

SOPEMI para 1976 – Bernard Kayser. In Ferreira, ES (ed) *A Emigração Portuguesa e o seu Contexto Internacional.* Centro de Estudos da dependência. Lisboa: Iniciativas Editoriais.

Stone, S and Desai, N (1989) *The Naughty Mouse.* London: Mantra

Swain, M (1972) *Bilingualism as a First Language.* Irvine: University of California, PhD Dissertation

Taylor, M (1987) *Chinese Pupils in Britain.* Windsor: National Foundation for Education Research

The London Reading Test (1992) Slough: NFER Nelson Publishing Company

Thomas, W and Collier, V (1997) *School Effectiveness for Language Minority Students.* IEP Symposium 22/23 May, London

Thomas, WP and Collier, V (1997) *School Effectiveness for Language Minority Children.* Washington. National Clearinghouse for Bilingual Education. <http://www.ncbe.gwu.edu>

Thomas, WP and Collier, V (2002). *A National Study of School Effectiveness for Language Minority Students' Long-Term Academic Achievement.* Center for Research on Education, Diversity and Excellence (CREDE). <http://www.crede.ucsc.edu.research/llaa/1.1_final.html>

Tollefson, JW (ed) (1995) *Power and Inequality in Language Education.* Cambridge: Cambridge University Press

TTA (2003) *Qualifying to Teach: Professional Standards for Qualified Teacher Status and Requirements for Initial Teacher Training.* Teacher Training Agency, London

Tomlinson, S (1984) *Home and School in Multicultural Britain*. London: Batsford Academic and Educational

Tomlinson, S (2000) Ethnic minorities and education: new disadvantages. In T Cox (ed) *Combating Educational Disadvantage*. London: Falmer Press

Tomlinson, S and Hutchison, S (1991) *Bangladeshi Parents and Education in Tower Hamlets*. An ACE-University of Lancaster Research Project

Topping, KJ (1986) *Parents as Educators*. Cambridge: Croom Helm

Trueba, HT, Guthrie, GP and Au, KH (eds) (1981) *Culture and the Bilingual Classroom: studies in classroom ethnography*. Rowley, Mass: Newbury House

van Lier, L (2000) From input to affordance: social-interactive learning from an ecological perspective. In JP Lantolf (ed) *Sociocultural Theory and Second Language Learning*. Oxford: Oxford University Press (p245-259)

Verhoeven, L (1987) *Ethnic Minority Children Acquiring Literacy*. Dordrecht: Foris

Verhoeven, L (1991) Acquisition of Biliteracy. In JH Hulsijn and JF Matter (eds) *Reading in Two Languages*. Amsterdam: AILA

Verhoeven, L (1994) Transfer in Bilingual Development. *Language Learning* 44(3) p381-415

Verhoeven, L (1999) Second language reading. In DA Wagner, RL Venezky and BV Street (eds) *Literacy, an International Handbook*. Oxford: Westview Press

Verma, G, Zec, P and Skinner, G (1994) *The Ethnic Crucible: harmony and hostility in multi-ethnic schools*. London: Falmer Press

Volk, D and deAcosta, M (2003) Reinventing texts and contexts: syncretic literacy events in young Puerto Rican children's homes. *Research in the Teaching of English* 38(1) p8-48

Wang, B (1982) Chinese children in Britain. (unpublished paper from Conference on Multi-ethnic Education, College of St Peter and St Paul, Cheltenham)

Watson, JL (1977) *Between Two Cultures: migrants and minorities in Britain*. Oxford: Basil Blackwell

Wells, G (1986) *The Meaning Makers*. London: Hodder and Stoughton

Winterson, J (2004) *Lighthousekeeping*. London: Harper Collins Publishers

Wong, LY (1992) *Education of Chinese children in Britain and the USA*. Clevedon: Multilingual Matters

Wu, CJ (2006) Look who's talking: language choices and culture of learning in UK Chinese classrooms. *Language and Education* 20(1) p62-75

INDEX